HUNDRED HINDU TEMP

ANCIENT, MEDIEVAL

C000050658

SANMUGAM ARUMUGAM

Edited by:
Thirumugam Arumugam

First Published as two books: 'Ancient Hindu Temples of Sri Lanka' in 1980 and 'More Hindu Temples of Sri Lanka' in 1991.

This combined edition published in 2014 by Ohm Books, UK

© 2014 Thirumugam Arumugam

ISBN 978-0-9575023-4-5

A CIP catalogue record for this book is available from the British Library.

Cover design by Darshan Rajarayan

INTRODUCTION TO 2014 EDITION

In 1980, Sanmugam Arumugam (1905 - 2000) wrote a book titled 'Ancient Hindu Temples of Sri Lanka'. There was a good demand for the book and a second revised edition was published in 1982. This second edition had two additional maps giving the locations of the temples and an Appendix giving details of the original Patrons of the temples. A Glossary of Tamil terms relating to temples was also included.

Encouraged by the warm reception accorded to the book, Sanmugam Arumugam wrote a second book which was published in 1991. It was titled 'More Hindu Temples of Sri Lanka'. The book gave details of additional ancient, medieval and modern Hindu Temples in Sri Lanka. Together, these two books contain details of over 100 Hindu Temples in Sri Lanka.

These two books have been out of print for quite a while, but there appears to be a continuing and growing interest in the subject. It was therefore considered worthwhile reprinting the two books, merging the contents of the two books into a single volume. The texts of the two books were written twenty-five to thirty-five years ago, so it is possible that some of the temples described have new buildings constructed in them since the text was written.

The beautiful hand-drawn sketch on the front cover has been drawn by Darshan RajaRayan, grandson of Sanmugam Arumugam. It is a sketch of the five-tiered Gopuram of the Thiruketheswaram Temple, which is near Mannar. The sketch used as a guideline the photograph of this Gopuram which is in the text of the book. Dharshan was also responsible for the cover design.

Thanks are also due to our publishers, Ohm Books and to Seggy T Segaran. If not for his enthusiasm, initiative and ebullience this volume would not have seen the light of day.

Thirumugam Arumugam
Sydney Australia
May 2014

CONTENTS

SECTION V: SAKTHI TEMPLES

Other Amman Kovils

SECTION VI: OTHER TEMPLES   225

PREFACE to Second Edition of 'Ancient Hindu Temples of Sri Lanka'

It had been my long-time desire to compile my notes and photographs, into a single volume, of the temples and shrines, where the Lords Grace had enabled me to make my obeisance in worship, during my active years.

This pleasant work commenced in 1971 but was however soon laid aside due to pre-occupation with the preparation of a detailed narrative of the 'Lord of Thiruketheeswaram'. When it was resumed again in 1978, it was intended to confine its scope to places of worship less well known today, but known to have existed before the advent of the foreign powers in Ceylon. However, other temples were also added including recent structures where I had been personally associated. Each group of temples has been arranged commencing from Jaffna, proceeding outwards.

I have found C. S. Navaratnam's book on 'A Short History of Hinduism in Ceylon', very valuable.

In the Second Edition, the text has been revised, two Maps, an informative Appendix and a Glossary also added. Chronology has been amended at places, due to recent conclusions

S. ARUMUGAM.
4/71, Polhengoda Road, Colombo 5.
1981

INTRODUCTION to 'Ancient Hindu temples of Sri Lanka'

'The Tamil races were perhaps the greatest temple builders in the World' Encyclopaedia Brittanica 9th. Edition

Hindu religious worship may either be private, at home in the domestic set-up, or be public, at a temple, where several are present and where the ceremonies are performed by the priest. In the 'Tholka-pium', we find references to Murugan, deity of the mountain tops, Thirumal and the Vedic Gods, Indra, Varuna, Sun, Moon and Fire. The attributes of Lord Siva are referred to in Sangam literature. The temple was the focal centre of the social and cultural activities of the people. These had to encompass, within their precincts, halls for schools and other scholastic activities, reference libraries, facilities for feeding, conference halls and halls for musical and dance performances. The King has to have a Raja Mandapam. So we get the gradual evolution of the traditional features of a temple structure.

Temple Architecture

The concept of a shrine or temple, a place or building, where several can assemble and congregate appears to have existed during the Vedic times as the Rig Veda (81.4) mentions even the kind of wood that had to be used to build these temples. Thus the concept could be assigned to the era of years 1500 to 1000 B.C. Due however to the perishable nature of timber it was gradually replaced with materials of a more permanent nature, such as the rock. Temples of structural stone, as different from earlier structures in rock architecture were the work of the Pallavas in the 7th century. The Chola period inherited and continued the Pallava tradition in temple construction. Many of the features that are seen today were introduced. The simple sikharam of old was replaced with a multi-tiered Vimanam, with the semi-circular dome or present day Sthoopy, with a Kalasam crowning the top. Walls were ornamented with sculptured pilasters; the facades had vyala maddam, as an intermediate terminal stage; the cornice was decorated with kudus.

The Pandya regime devoted attention to the architectural embellishments of the exterior of the temple structure; the erection of the high multi-tiered Gopurams at entrances to temples is their unique feature. Addition of outer mandapams and provision of more prahara murthy shrines were also their contribution. The simple pillar became more ornamental; the corbel was moulded to represent more closely the plantain bunch flower type of pendant. This became even sharper later with the Nayakas in the Madurai ornamentations. These are the architectural features of a Hindu Temple Structure.

Symbolism and Functions

The Hindu Temple, says K. Navaratnam, is so constructed as to resemble the structure of the human body. It resembles the body of a man lying on his back with the head in the West and the feet towards the East.

Head	Garbagraham
Neck	Artha Mandapam
Chest	Maha Mandapam
Stomach	Sthapana Mandapam
Section below the intestines	Sthampa Mandapam
Thighs	Sabha Mandapam
Knees	First entrance
Lower Legs	Kalyana Mandapam or Utsava Mandapam
Feet	Main entrance with Gopuram

The main image or the Mula Murthy is installed in the Garba Graham. The Utsava Murthies (functional images) are placed in the Maha Mandapam. In the human body, the functional organs are in the chest above the stomach. The sacrificial pit is constructed in the Sthapana Mandapam into which offerings of rice and ghee are made during 'Homa'. The flagstaff Kodi Sthampam and the Pali Pedam are in the Sthampa Mandapam. Music and Dances are performed in the Sabha Mandapam. The Utsava Murthy is decorated and placed in the Kalyana Mandapam during festival days. The first entrance with a small gopuram represents the knees. The big gopuram on the main entrance represents the feet with the toes up. 'The shrine for the Sakthi aspect of the Maha Murthy (Chief Deity) is placed on the Northern side of the Maha Mandapam facing south. The tall tower over the Garbagraham is called the Vimanam or Sthoopi and towers at the entrances of the temple are called Gopurams '.

Hindu Temples in Sri Lanka

There are a large number of Hindu Temples in Sri Lanka today particularly in the North and the East. Some of them are of very ancient origin; many of them belong to the medieval era, however all are grouped together, for convenience. The story of how these temples came to be founded and how personages came to erect temples for their worship is of great interest.

Events said to have been enacted in nebulous eras have been perpetuated by devotees by the subsequent erection of temples at the locations. Such are Thiruketheeswaram (temple No. 30 in this book), Koneswaram, No. 31 and Muneswaram, No. 33. Vijaya the first King of Lanka is reported to have restored these Iswaran temples dedicated to the worship of Parameswaran.

Velautha (Kandasamy) shrines of the Eastern littoral region are said to be of Veddah origin and are associated with events in the Puranic war of God Skanda with the asura Sura Pathman. Later, they were built as temples such as Nos: 58, 59, 61, 62 and 63.

In the second century, King Gaja Bahu, as described on page 211, introduced the Pattini cult and several temples for Pattini Devi and Kannakai Amman were founded in Lanka. In the North, many of these have now become Amman Kovils for Rajarajeswari Ambal Nagambal and Muttumari Ambal. Temple No. 96. Panri Thalachchi and Vaththapalai No. 97 are two foremost Kannakai Amman Kovils, today.

Pallava tradition and culture was widely prevalent in the sixth and seventh centuries. Their religious resurgence had far reaching effects on the development of Hinduism in this country. Existing temples were renovated and several newly erected. Thevaram song offerings by saints Thiru Gnana Sambanthar and Suntharar exalt the celebrated temple Nos: 30 and 31 to the status of padal petra sthalams.

The Cholas, who were in Lanka from the year 985 to 1070, had Polonnaruwa as their principal city. Ruins of sixteen Hindu temples have now been unearthed in eight groups. Some of them are described in detail under temple No. 36. Many excellent Chola bronze icons have also been found. These remind us of the excellence of Hindu Temple architecture and superb art attained in the 11th and 12th centuries.

The temple at Thirukovil No. 63 and Koneswaram No. 31, retain today remnants of the Pandyan edifices that were there long ago.

Hindu temples gained prominence early in the thirteenth century due to King Magha. Kalinga Magha (Makon) was sent by his father principally to promote Saivaism and to be interested particularly in the Eastern parts of the Island. He fulfilled these, by setting up the regime of the Vanniyars, who were very religious. Several temples in the Northern and the Eastern Vanni regions remind us today of the deep interest the Vanni Chieftans had taken to promote Saivaism.

The Singai Ariyans of the Jaffna Kingdom, with the names Sekarajasekaram and Pararajasekaram, ruled as independant Ariyachakravarti Kings of Jaffna from about the year 1284 onwards. They, of course, were deeply interested in promoting Hinduism and are known to have erected temples No. 2, 3, 4, 5, 8, 23, 55, 90 and several others. In fact one of the Kings is reported to have paid homage at every temple in his little kingdom, founding more where needed.

Most of the Hindu temples in Sri Lanka were destroyed by foreign invaders in the 16th and the 17th centuries. The architectural edifices erected by our ancient Royalty are now no more. What we see today are the less pretentious structures bearing the original names, put up subsequently, by the people themselves.

A temple structure, finished in detail, keeping with traditonal Dravidian temple architecture of the Vijayanagara School, is the recently erected Ponnambalavaneswarar Temple, No. 35, in Colombo.

Review of First Edition of 'Ancient Hindu Temples of Sri Lanka'

Here is a praiseworthy performance of an ardent devotee who has made good use of his pilgrimages during the period of his official duties all over the Island. Shri S. Arumugam was senior Deputy Director of Irrigation when he retired from Government Service after thirty years of active participation.

In this context it will be relevant to refer to the literary contributions of civil servants of the past, mostly Englishmen who collected all available particulars of the historical events in the places where they had worked. Their publications have been useful to students of research.

Shri S. Arumugam has prefaced his book with very useful introductory notes on the pattern of a Hindu Temple describing the evolution and symbolism of the structure.

The illustrations and the foot-notes that are mostly reference to earlier books on this subject make the reader sustain his enthusiasm for reading this book right up to the end and adding to his own knowledge.

This is another welcome publication that should find its way into the shelves of Public Libraries here and in other parts of the world where the medium of understanding is in English.

The compilation, the features and the general presentation of this edition must be commended.

Extract from the 'Hindu Organ' of 25-7-1980.

PREFACE to 'More Hindu Temples of Sri Lanka'

'Some Ancient Hindu Temples of Sri Lanka' was first published in 1980 and reprinted in 1982. Encouraged by the warm reception accorded to that work, a second compilation has now been made of a few more temples, including some in ruins and some now extant.

I express my gratitude to Rajadurai for valuable assistance with the illustrations of both this and the earlier works. The more recent views are the excellent work of Rajkumar Rajarayan.

To the many who appreciated the earlier work and urged me on, my grateful thanks.

S. Arumugam
London, 1990

INTRODUCTION to 'More Hindu temples of Sri Lanka'

The Tamils are known to have been great Temple Builders through the ages. The magnificent temples of India bear evidence today of the splendour of the Tamil civilisation and Hindu Culture. Hinduism has been aptly said to be a way of life and religious culture of the Tamils is exemplified in the erection of stupendous edifices.

Unfortunately no imposing Hindu monument survives today in Sri Lanka. The foreign powers, who demolished these edifices in the seventeenth century, did their work so thoroughly that even the foundations had been eradicated and the stones taken for building Forts elsewhere. Moreover at some of these, other buildings have been erected. The erection of even new temples at the very site of the ancient location deprives posterity of any chance of examining the precious legacy of the past.

Because of these factors, the Hindu generation of today is deprived of extensive tangible evidence of their glorious past culture; they have to be content with scanty relics, damaged inscriptions, and some references at a few places. Even these are mostly bare. My interest in many of these is largely due to seeing them personally, during my active years when searching for ancient irrigation works out in the jungles. The striking feature is that many ruins are found in the midst of, so to say, nowhere, in the interior of the jungles. Yet the fascination of delving into the past leads to enchantment; no sensation is greater than seeing a lost or broken down temple, which would have been once a thriving place of love, piety and adoration of multitudes.

An effort has been made in this compilation to cite some of those that had come to my knowledge. These show how religious culture was fostered by the Tamils in Sri Lanka during the past. Today, it is possible to visit a few of them, some are not to be found; a few have been rebuilt but others allowed to decay.

It is realised not many readers would get the chance to make their obeisance before all these Hindu Sthalams of 'once upon a time'; yet it is hoped that religious and cultural sentiment will be sufficiently stimulated with a craving to pay homage at most of them.

Recollection of the glorious past and an awareness of the present could inspire the building of a bright future.

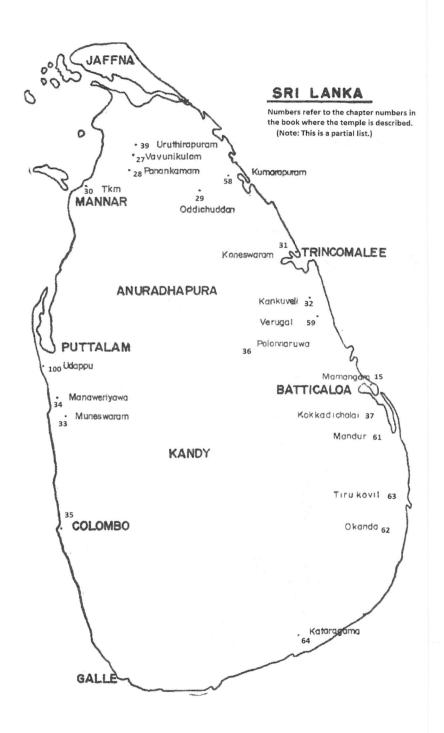

JAFFNA

SRI LANKA

Numbers refer to the chapter numbers in
the book where the temple is described.
(Note: This is a partial list.)

39 Uruthirapuram
27 Vavunikulam
28 Panankamam   Kumarapuram
                58
30 Tkm   29
MANNAR   Oddichuddan

                      31 TRINCOMALEE
            Koneswaram

ANURADHAPURA

            Kankuveli 32
            Verugal   59
            Polonnaruwa
         36

                    Mamangam 15
            BATTICALOA

            Kokkadicholai 37
            Mandur 61

PUTTALAM
100 Udappu

    Manaweriyawa
34 Muneswaram
33

        KANDY

                    Tirukovil 63

35   Okanda 62
COLOMBO

                    Kataragama
                64

GALLE

16

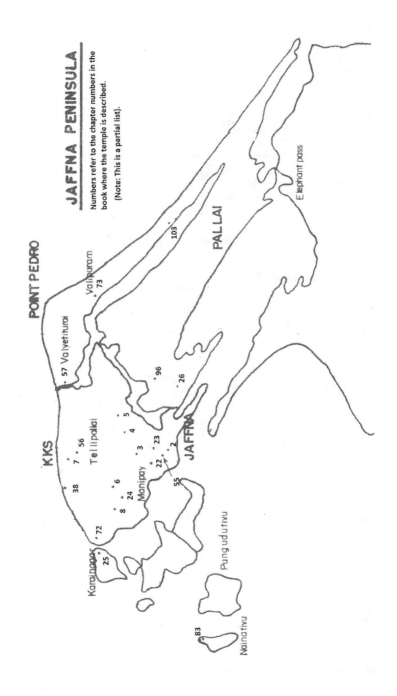

JAFFNA PENINSULA

Numbers refer to the chapter numbers in the book where the temple is described.

(Note: This is a partial list).

POINT PEDRO

Valvettiturai

57 Valvettiturai

Vaittaram
73

103

PALLAI

Elephant pass

KKS

96

26

7 56

Tellippalai

5

4

3

23

JAFFNA

38

6

22

2

24

Manipay

55

8

72

Pungudutivu

Karainagar

25

83

Nainativu

17

SECTION 1

VINAYAKAR TEMPLES

1. VENERATION OF VINAYAKAR

Worship of Vinayaka Murthi is wide spread in Sri Lanka. He is revered by Hindus and Buddhists as well. His other names are Ganesa, Ganapathy, Vigneswara, Pillaiyar and Yanaimukan. Vinayaka is the God of Wisdom. His origin is difficult to trace; there are of course several legends of his birth. It is believed that the veneration of Vinayakar by the Hindus commenced about the 5th century, probably with the Vatapi Expedition.

Vinayakar thwarts all obstacles therefore his worship is accorded the first place in all Hindu ceremonies both in the Temple and in the home. Even the Celestial Beings are said to have worshipped this 'Remover of Obstacles', before embarking on any important undertaking.

His Representation

Hindu deities are represented through various symbols. Usually there are a 'mantra' (sound representation), a 'yantra' (graphic representation) and an 'icon' or image representation. Vinayaka's mantra is the utterance of the sacred single 'AUM'. His yantra is the Swastika.

The physical form of the image of Vinayakar is unique in concept. The elephant face and the heavy bearing are unusual but they are suggestive of immense power. He has only one whole tusk, the other is broken halfway. The long trunk bends at the end for getting around obstacles. Of the four arms the two lower arms are in the familiar abhaya (fear not) and boon giving poses. In one of the upper arms is a noose and in the other a hook. The noose is suggestive of his intention to remove delusion from his devotees and the hook is indicative of his position as leader or ruler.

His Vahana or vehicle

How a little mouse can be a vehicle for an elephant-like figure is of course not easy to understand. The combination however serves to depict symbolically the immensity of the Divine to the humble human. Rodents are also well known to be capable of gnawing their way through obstacles and the mouse may symbolically indicate overcoming of obstacles.

As if in explanation of why one of the tusks is broken, there is an interesting legend which is often depicted in pictures. As the sage Viyasa narrated the story of the Mahabharatha, Vinayaka is said to have written it down; but at a certain stage the inscribing needle broke and Vinayaka promptly substituted part of one of his tusks.

Although the Vinayakar concept entered Hindu worship later than several other concepts of the Divine, yet Vinayakar Murthi is the popularly revered Hindu Deity in Sri Lanka today. It is easily possible to count over two hundred and fifty Vinayaka Temples and a similar number of Pillaiyar Temples; in addition there are hundreds of Shrines. Sithi Vinayakar is the most popular name; there are also Veerakathy, Katpaha, Maruthady and other Vinayakar Murthies.

As propitiating Vinayakar Murthy is auspicious for success of any undertaking, there is always a constant stream of worshippers at a Pillaiyar temple.

Ancient Temples.

Several ancient Vinayakar Murthi statues have been unearthed, some of which are described here and later under the respective Temples.

Discovered at Thiruketheeswaram

Thiruketheeswaram is a celebrated sthalam of holy antiquity. The locality has a long history as a Hindu place of worship, venerated by devotees through the ages. The author's book on 'The Lord of Thiruketheeswaram' provides a detailed account of its ancient glory and its venerated history.

Among the statues of old, unearthed here is an ancient stone statue of Vinayakar Murthi. It had attracted much attention due to its skilled workmanship and has been commented upon as belonging to the Pallava period of Hindu Culture.

Ancient Ganesa vigrakam unearthed near Thiruketheeswaram Temple.
It inspired the Saiva Saints of the 7th century.

It is given a special place in the Maha Mandapam of the present temple at Thiruketheeswaram where it receives priority in the puja ceremonies.

In the picture may be seen the Vinayaka Vigrakam installed at the temple and also in sketch form, what the late Shanmuganathan, Asst. Arch. Commissioner made of it, when he was making a special study of same.

Sketch drawn by S. Sanmuganathan

Unearthed at Trincomalee

An impressive bronze Vinayaka Murthi vigraham was unearthed, along with other 'finds', at Trincomalee in the year 1950.

Massive bronze Vinayaka Murthi statue unearthed in Trincomalee, 1950.
Now installed in Koneswaram temple. Probably of the Pandyan era.

Vinayaka is seen in a standing pose: much credit has been given to the sthapathy artist who has skillfully depicted Ganesa, 'the elephant-headed deity, who has the strength of an elephant and wisdom of a man'. Weighing 65 lbs, it is massive and is said to have high gold content.

Reference:

Balendra, Dr. W., 'Trincomalee Bronzes' P. 12

2. KAILAYA NATHA PILLAIYAR TEMPLE, NALLUR, JAFFNA

I have been associated with this temple from my infancy and have walked about the temple yard for years, from the period when Sri La Sri Cumaraswamy Kurukkal was the chief priest. Since then, he has been succeeded by his son and then by his grandson and now (1979) by his great grandson.

The Kailaya Malai has presented a record of how this temple came to be erected, by Kulangai Singai Aryan founder of the Greater Hindu Kingdom of Jaffna, as the first Ariya Chakravarti. Arriving from Madurai, in S. India, he made Nallur the capital of his new Saivite Kingdom of Jaffna. At the behest of Kailaya Nathar (Lord Shiva and Parvathy Ambal) in a dream, he set about building a beautiful edifice for the Lord. Special priests performed the Kumba-abishekam ceremonies *. 'The floor of the temple was smeared with fragrant sandal paste and there a throne of great splendour set with rubies, blue sapphires, cat's eyes, diamonds and pearls was placed.... At last the priest took the golden pot filled with holy water and poured it over the images and consecrated them in the midst of great roar of musical trumpets, drums of various kinds, praises, songs and hymns and called Siva by the name of Kailayanatha and invoked him to the image '.

(* *Kailaya Malai is an ancient work written by Muthurasan, son of Sandiappan of Chola Country.*

The historian A. Mootoothamby Pillai has presented extracts from it in the Ceylon National Review of January 1907, which had been quoted in the 'Hindu Organ' of 31.5.1968.

Yalpana Vaipava Malai is the chronicle of Jaffna history. Maiylvagana Pulavar, descendant of the hereditary bards of the Kings of Jaffna, wrote this in the year 1736 at the behest of Maccra, Dutch Governor of Ceylon. He obtained his material from the Kailya Malai, Rasa Murai and other chronicles now extinct. A new edition has been published by Kula Sabanathan in 1953.)

The King lived in splendour and his Nallur Kingdom is said to have been another Kailayam on earth. He was succeeded by his son Kulasekara Singai Aryan and so the progeny ensued.

The beautiful structure that Singai Maha Raja built was destroyed about 400 years later on the 2nd of February 1620 when the Kingdom of Jaffna fell to the Portuguese. It is said that when the temple was about to be destroyed the chief priest, fled to his native village of Madduvil, taking with him the Moorthy Vigrakams which he dropped into the temple ponds there. Years later the Lingam was recovered and housed in the Madduvil Sivan Temple.

A few years later, the Dutch who were in Jaffna from 1658 to 1796, were salvaging the stones from the once great Kailaya Natha Temple, for building their great sea 'Fort Hammenheil' (now in ruins), off Kayts. The villagers finding the statue of a Pillaiyar in the debris placed it under a vilva tree, for worship. Arumuga Navalar erected a cadjan shed over the Vinayaka statue, in 1850, making it a shrine. His nephew T. Kailasapillai improved the shed into a permanent masonry building and the structure became known as Kailaya Pilliayar Kovil, with Vinayaka Moorthy presiding in it, functioning under the trusteeship of the descendants of T. Kailasapillai, of the Navalar line, viz, P. Ramalingam and thence to others.

Coming now to years within my personal knowledge, I remember a general desire among Pillaiyar's devotees, that the temple should also house a Siva Lingam and an Ambal, for, was it not the abode of Kailaya Nathar and Parvathy Ambal, when the original edifice was erected by the first Ariyachakravarti arasan in the 13th Century?

With a lead given by the progeny of Madurai Appah (an elder from Nallur, known for his devotion, who took up residence at Madurai for devotional work), C. Suntheram, who held an important government position, spear-headed a movement for rebuilding the temple structure, improving it by paving the floor with granite slabs and to include a Siva sthalam in addition. On the unfortunate demise of C. Sunderam in 1924, his sister Manicka Ammaiyar, widow of Sabapathy Mudaliyar, continued with the undertaking, with the help of others. The chief priest Cumaraswamy Kurukal, a most devoted person, was a great asset to the functioning of the temple. The work came to a completion by 1946, when Kumba-abishekam ceremonies were performed. With the installation of a Siva Lingam and Ambal and other prahara Moorthies, the Kailaya Pillaiyar Temple was named Kailaya Natha Pillaiyar Kovil. The Ammaiyar had the satisfaction of seeing her task completed within her life time, before her demise in 1962.

On the demise of Cumaraswamy Kurukkal, chief priest, his son Kurusamy Kurukkal succeeded him; upon his demise he was succeede by his eldest son Sharma Kurukkal.

Manimandapam for the Ther

The construction of a wooden Ther, commenced during the lifetime of Manicka Ammaiyar was completed by her brother S. Somasunderam assisted by her relations, in 1963. C. Sunderalingam was chiefly responsible for the erection of a majestic structure to house the new Ther.

Continuing his interest in the temple, he made arrangements for the installation of a special vigraham, the Pancha Muga Pillaiyar (five-headed Vinayaka moorthy), which is housed in the western praharam (south-west corner), An additional vasal (front entrance) enables the worshipping of the moorthy from outside, so that the Kailaya Natha Pillaiyar temple of today is adorned with a triple vasal frontal entrance.

Kailaya Natha Pillaiyar Temple, Nallur - the triple entrance

Regular daily pujas are performed at the temple. Annual festivals are held in April for Pillaiyar and in June for Kailaiya Nathar.

3. PARARAJASEKARA PILLAIYAR TEMPLE, INUVIL, JAFFNA

Kanagasuriyam was a celebrated king, who ruled the kingdom of Jaffna from Nallur, as King Pararajasekaram from the year 1478 to 1519 These forty one years were the Golden Age of the Jaffna Kingdom. The King's brother Segarajasekaram, a scholar of repute, encouraged learning and culture. Pararajasekaram was himself a scholar and a pious King. He paid homage at all the temples in his little kingdom, had the celebrated four temples of Nallur renovated, and built new temples for the well-being of his subjects.

Pararajasekara Pillaiyar Temple: Recently erected Raja Gopuram

One of the temples of his period, we have today, is the Pararajasekara Pillaiyar Temple at Inuvil. Built by Royal Command on the orders of the king, it must have been a grand structure and would have enjoyed the patronage of the Royal Household and the civic population of the kingdom.

Unfortunately like all Hindu temples of the period, tragedy overcame it, when it suffered destruction at the hands of the foreign invaders in the sixteenth century. However, with the renaissance of Hinduism in the nineteenth century, the Pillaiyar temple has been restored by leading personages and elders of the place.

Prominent names, in connection with the rebuilding, are K. Nadarajah Kurukkal, P. Ambikaipahar school master, and that of Maylar Arumugam. The outstanding bell tower that we see in the illustration is a contribution made by S. Thurairajah, while T. Nagamuttu and others were responsible for an exquisite ratham (ther). A major contribution made to Vinayakar recently is the magnificent Raja Gopuram completed, as a result of the untiring efforts of S. Appiah Pillai, in 1972. This prominent five-tiered structure is seen in the illustration. We thus have today a grand Pillaiyar temple with large mandapams, to remind us of the days of the Nallur Kings.

Prahara moorthy shrines adorn the inner veedy. Devotees pay obeisance to the Pancha Muga Pillaiyar, Lakshmi Ambal, Subramaniya Moorthy and other deities there.

The annual festivals are celebrated in the month of May; the Ther festival is one of special occurrence when three rathams are taken out in procession, and the large numbers of worshippers are blessed by tharisanam of Vinayakar and Subramaniya Moorthies.

4. KARUNAKARA PILLAIYAR TEMPLE, URUMPIRAI, JAFFNA

The Karunakara Pillaiyar temple at Urumpirai is an ancient temple. This temple is popularly associated with Karunakara Thondaiman, who is said to have been a distinguished General under King Kulatunga Cholan I (1070-1118 AC). The General had been sent from India for the development and procurement of salt in the Karanavai tracts in the Jaffna Peninsula. While living at Inuvil, a neighbouring village, he is said to have been a keen devotee of this temple; he may have probably founded it. We find mention of this in 'Ancient Jaffna' by Mudaliyar C. Rasanayagam. The 'Yalppana Vaipava Malai' records the event of Thondaiman excavating the Thondaiman Aru, a sea outlet for marine transport from the interior.

Karunakara Pillaiyar Temple, Urumpirai
(The author contemplating the past)

This temple enjoys an important unique feature; of all the temples in the Jaffna Peninsula this is the only temple where a **stone inscription** has so far been found, relating to it. The only other temple where there is a stone inscription is the Nagapooshani Ambal Kovil at Nainativu, but there the inscription relates to a feature not connected with the temple.

This temple is also associated, by local tradition, with (Kulangai) Singai Ariyan, the first of the Ariya Chakravarti Kings of Jaffna, a reputed temple builder, who went about paying homage at every temple in his little kingdom, and founding more where needed.

Enjoying the reputation of having been sponsored earlier by distinguished personages and backed with Royal support, the temple would have had its glorious period during the days of the Kings of Jaffna prior to the arrival of the foreign powers. The dark years of the seventeenth century saw the demolition of several Hindu temples in Jaffna and this temple was no exception. Local folks claim even today that the demolition party, having broken up the temple structure was unable to carry away the blessed Vinayaka Thiru Vadivam as He willed it otherwise.

Whatever that may be, the fact remains that years later, with the dawn of the Hindu renaissance in Jaffna and the Navalar Era, one Karunakara Iyer reinstituted Vinayakar worship at the site.

The development and growth of the present Karunakara Pillaiyar temple structure is largely due to the devotion and tireless efforts of the priests who for generations officiated as Kurukkals at the temple.

After Karunakara Iyer there was Parama Iyer and then Appu Kutty Iyer during whose lifetime the temple structure assumed traditional shape with Maha Mandapam. His son Vaitheespara Kurukkal, a learned person of outstanding quality and merit brought the temple to a leading position. Now his son Sabaretna Kurukkal is maintaining its traditions.

Nadarajah Shrine Sthoopy at above Temple

We therefore have today a well maintained Hindu Vinayakar temple where pujas are devotedly performed according to Saiva agamic rites and requirements. Embodied in

29

the temple is a Nadarajah Shrine, in which are housed the Nadarajah Thiru Vadivam and the Arumuga Swamy Vigrakam.

The Inscription

The inscription or rather two inscriptions are found on a eleven inch by eleven inch square stone about thirty eight inches long. The inscription reads continuously on all four sides of the stone and occupies about half its length. The other half was probably left for burying or embedding into the ground. Prof. K. Indrapala had been given the opportunity by the temple authorities to carefully inspect and read the inscription. He has contributed an article, on his findings, to the temple 'Kumba Abisheka Malar', published in 1973, from which this material has been obtained.

This stone, it is said, used to be outside the temple until the days of Vaitheespara Kurukkal who took steps to take it into the sanctum, where it is now an object of veneration. It was first inspected by Mudaliyar C. Rasanayagam, who gave his opinion in 'Ancient Jaffna' (1928) that it narrated to Karunakara Pillaiyar temple and that it was inscribed in the year 1567. Prof. Indrapala first saw it in 1962 but later during the reconstruction of the temple in 1973 was able to have the stone taken out to make a closer and detailed scrutiny.

The first inscription consists of eleven lines and is inscribed in Tamil language of the 16th century commencing with 'Iswasthy Sri' greeting. No names of Kings or rulers are mentioned but the year 'Pirapava' and month 'Sithirai' - are readable. This inscription dated April 1567 records the names (obliterated) of donors of a gift, probably of land, to the Karunakara Pillaiyar Temple. The inscription concludes with the poignant rendering that anyone who violates this gift shall incur sins equivalent to killing the sacred cow on the banks of the river Ganges. Considering the Vairava Soolam inscribed on it, it is surmised that it could be a boundary stone.

The second inscription which appears above the first is shorter, consisting of five lines only. It has been considered to be of a later date, estimated to be about the end of the sixteenth century. It records the donation of five panams to the temple Pandaram.

We can visualise today with deep feeling, the anguish of the engravers and others connected with the affairs of the temple at the time these inscriptions were made. Dark clouds were amassing on the horizon and evil happenings threatened everywhere. History tells us of the tragic years for temples.

Tragedy occurs in Mannar (1544), Jaffna is invaded (1560), Mannar is captured (1561), Sangily dies (1565), Muneswaram temple is destroyed (1575) and pujas terminate at Thiruketheeswaram (1589); devastation and demolition of other temples followed.

Temple Society

A Society was formed in 1959 to look after the affairs of the temple and eminent persons of the locality hold leading positions in the Society. Since then, many additions and improvements have been done to the temple building. A new structure was erected to house the Ther in 1965.

Annual Festivals

The annual festival commences with Aavany Sathurthi in August and lasts for ten days. During the concluding ratham festival devotees gather here from all parts of Jaffna for tharisanam of Karunakara Vinayaka Moorthy.

Reference:

'Kumba Abisheka Malar' in Tamil, published by the Temple authorities in 1973.

5. ARASAKESARI PILLAIYAR TEMPLE, NEERVELY, JAFFNA

This temple is situated about a mile to the west of the sixth mile-post on the Jaffna-Pt. Pedro road. It bears the name of a distinguished person of the court of Pararajasekaram, King of Jaffna (1478-1519). Pararajasekaram was one of the most successful Kings of Jaffna and during his reign art, learning and culture flourished. The King's brother Segarajasekeram, an eminent scholar, invited poets and learned people from India and held discourses. Arasakesari, a nephew of the King was an eminent Sanskrit scholar who translated Kalidasa's Sanskrit classic titled 'Raguwamsam' into Tamil. He is said to have done this, sitting on the banks of the Nayan Mar Kaddu Kulam in Nallur. There was yet another Arasakesari who ruled as Regent from 1615 to 1617, but met with an untimely death.

Arasakerari Pillaiyar Temple, Neervely

A publication made by A. S. Cumaraswamy, a copy of which is available with the chief priest Sri Samba Sathasiva Kurukkal of the temple, relates how this temple was founded. During the era mentioned above, when the Nallur-Neervely region enjoyed its golden age, it was revealed in a dream that there was a spring situated on the 'Rasa Veethy', the waters of which were a very sacred theertham. The King had the 'Rasa Veethy', a roadway running North from Nallur, examined and the sacred spring located, and a 'theertham' built. By the side, of course a Vinayaka temple was also founded. But the celebrated Arasakesari Pillaiyar Kovil of that era, which enjoyed Royal patronage, has all been lost, due to demolition by foreign invaders in the seventeenth century.

However, subsequently, in 1800, it is said, that one Kadirgamar Iyampillai took the initiative to build a shrine of some sort which later in 1873, Sri Cumarasamy Kurukkal, grand father of the present Kurukkal made into a proper agamic Vinayakar Kovil. A Board of Trustees took charge of the temple in 1949 and has made several improvements and additions. An elaborate ornamental Gopura Vasal, found at the entrance, was constructed in 1959. The temple is often referred to as 'Sempaddu Pillaiyar Kovil'.

Apart from the Moolasthana Vinayaka Moorthy, there are shrines of the sacred Siva Lingam and Ambal, Subramaniyar, Navakgrahams and also of course of Bhairavar.

The temple is well administered today and regular pujas and other observances are made and monthly Sathurthi festivals held. The annual festival commences with the aavany sathurthy in August and continues for 12 days.

A notable feature is that the above 'theertham' occupies the sixth place in a long list of sacred theerthams of the Island.

6. MARUTHADY PILLAIYAR TEMPLE, MANIPAY, JAFFNA

The Maruthady Pillaiyar temple is located by the main road from Jaffna to Chankanai, opposite the Green Memorial Hospital at Manipay. Its unique feature is that it has entrances both in the East and the West, and its moolasthanam faces west.

Like all places of public worship, the exact date of its origin is not known. The temple story 'Aalaya Manmiam' (1925) makes references to the pulling down of a temple which stood at the site, by the Portuguese. Local tradition holds the belief that the place became holy and reverential as an eminent savant who came from India lived there and spent his last days at the site, in the olden days.

Whatever that may have been, it is fairly well established that Vinayakar worship was commenced here by a venerable Thiyagarajah Saiva Kurukkal. The Kurukkal, it is said, first settled down at Navaly but finding repugnant practices there, such as animal sacrifice at the Bhairava Shrine, moved on to this more congenial site, bringing with him the Vinayakar statue. This site was most becoming for worship, prayer and meditation as it was in a maruthamara grove by the banks of a Thirukulam. Many people gathered there for tharisanam of Vinayaka Moorthy, squatting at the foot of the Marutha tree and soon the shrine became a landmark for religious worship at Manipay.

With the increasing number of worshippers of Pillaiyar, and the activities of other religionists in the vicinity, the need for a permanent temple structure soon became evident and release of suitable land was secured in 1856 from the Government for the purpose. In this activity the name of Swaminatha Mudaliyar gains prominence. A permanent structure was soon erected. Sometime at this juncture, the Pillaiyar was also installed facing away from the road to avoid any awkward situations in view of a church building across the road.

The temple thus continues to function from that time onwards with the unique feature of having entrances both in the East and West, and drawing large crowds during the annual festival terminating with the Ther festival on Hindu New Year day.

7. KASATHURAI ANANDA PILLAIYAR TEMPLE, KANKESANTURAI

Almost opposite the Petrol Filling Station at Kankesanturai is a precious small temple, snug and sheltered by other buildings in the foreground. Its origin and history is most revealing. Named today as Kasathurai Ananda Pillaiyar or more often just Kankesanturai Pillaiyar, it has history going back several centuries.

Kasathurai Ananda Pillaiyar Temple, Kankesanturai

History tells us that Kankesanturai was once known as Gayaturai, in the ancient days. It was then the sea port where pilgrims embarked for travel to Gaya. It saw the celebrated landing of Kankeyan, the Skanda Vikraham of immortal fame for installation at the new temple Marutha Pira Valli had completed in the ninth century. With that, it came to be referred to as Kankesanturai.

But in the very olden days, when Gayaturai was handling pilgrim traffic, a learned sage by the name of Bavanantha Muniver, it is said, had installed at the site for his worship a Siva Lingam and the spot soon became a site of worship and veneration.

The sthalam became a place of heavenly solace and mental comfort to the departing pilgrims, as those were days when maritime travel involved untold hazard and danger. However, invoking Vinayakar, who wards off all dangers, gave them confidence and so the temple became popular. The temple also came to be referred to as 'Yathirai Pillaiyar', and a Pillaiyar Kovil it continues to be even today.

I was told when I went to make my obeisance to Vinayakar that the foot padam or the bottom of the original 'moorthy' extended more than six feet into the ground. Such was the sound work of the ancients.

However we worship him as Pillaiyar, as Vinayakar who would help us ward off all evils and hazards. The Vinayaka canopy in front assures us all these.

We read the story in a publicaton entitled 'Ananda Kanapathy' (in Tamil), published by the present trustee K. Arambamoorthy, in memory of his father A. Kathiripillai, who had managed the temple from 1914 to 1970.

8. PARALAI ISWARA VINAYAKAR TEMPLE, CHULIPURAM, JAFFNA

In the North-West region of the Jaffna Peninsula, close to the coastal area, there are two villages of ancient lore called Tholpuram and Chulipuram. Tholpuram means the settlement where ancient traditions prevail and Chulipuram is said to have generated from Choliapuram or the settlement of the Cholas. Tholpuram's proud possession is its Ponnalayam Vishnu Temple and Chulipuram has its ancient Paralai Vinayakar Kovil.

There exists a miraculous anecdote, handed to us by tradition, which makes the name of Paralai Pillaiyar, a treasure in the hearts of all Hindus.

Paralai Vinayakar Temple, Chulipuram

Built during the era of the Kings of Jaffna, the small Vinayakar temple existed before the Portuguese period. Tradition has it that when the Portuguese demolition party (several Hindu temples were broken down at that time) approached this temple, they were attacked by a flock of crows resulting in their leader losing his eyesight. This Divine intervention had won for the deity of the temple, the name of Kannai Koththy Kaththa Pillaiyar (the Pillaiyar who caused the crows to peck the eye), by which name He is referred to even today.

Whatever that may have been, this temple too suffered in the hands of the invaders. Later, at the time of resuscitation of Hinduism in Jaffna, it is known to have been rebuilt by one Nannithamby Murugesu. It would have been added on and renovated subsequently. Today we see the large mandapams and the many limestone masonry walls and pillars standing up.

Proper maintenance of the building would enchance the beauty of the temple which is so ideally situated in the midst of vast expanse of agricultural cultivation. Regular pujas are performed daily three times by the Poshager and the annual festival season is in June, after the festivities in the adjoining, and today's better known, Muruka Moorthy or Sri Sivasubramaniya Swami Kovil.

In the neighbourhood are several places of interest. The ancient sea port Sambuthurai, in the vicinity, has many historical associations. There is said to have been a Sivan Temple named Sambeswaran Kovil built by King Thissai Maluwan.

The region boasts of other places of historical interest. There is the celebrated Theertha sthalam of Thiru-adi-nilayam, or the place where Maha Vishnu's sacred foot trod. Today it is the location for theertha ceremonies of the deities from temples in the vicinity; the ocean there has become a frequented place for auspicious bathing and immersion of asthi.

An interesting revelation was made recently by Geologist Srimanne, when he was studying Ground Water conditions and behaviour in the entire Jaffna Peninsula. He showed me definite evidence of ground water escape underground to the sea at this place. Possibly that is how it has become a theertha sthalam.

Couple of miles away is the illustrious village of Matakal, meaning Mata-Kal, referring to the landing of an image of sacred Parvati Ambal.

Reference:

The location has become immortalised by 'Paralai Vinayakar Pallu', an old composition by a poet Nallur Sinnathamby, who lived during the days of the Dutch regime, near Saddanathar Kovil, Nallur, The work was first published in 1889 by Sivapragasa Pandithar, and has been reprinted since.

9. MURIKANDY PILLAIYAR SHRINE, MURIKANDY

Every traveller on the Jaffna-Kandy road makes obeisance to the Murikandy Pillaiyar, a way-side Vigneswara Shrine by the road-side near the 151 mile post, a few miles out from Kilinochchi. It is a well frequented spot; every vehicle that passes by stops and the occupants obtain dharshan of Vigneswara Moorthy before they proceed on their journey - for Vigneswara - his very name, assures us of the removal of all obstacles.

This humble shrine under a spreading tree (around which a good settlement has now sprung up), was meant really to indicate the original Murikandy, situated about 8 miles to the South-West in the interior. The roadside shrine was then referred to as Theru Murikandy.

Theru Murikandy Temple, 1980 on Jaffna - Kandy Road

The original or old Murikandy, as now referred to, is a well settled ancient village. Its muri (breached) kandy (swamp) has been built and is now majestic Murikandy Kulam.

It was old retired Vithanaiyar Sinnathurai of Kilinochchi (he was a colleague of Yoga Swamiyar, when both of them were working in the Irrigation Department), who made me visit (old) Murikandy village, sometime in the year 1949.

I met the elders of the village from whom I gathered a very interesting narrative of how the Murikandys (old and new) came to be established:

It was during the days when the Jaffna-Kandy roadway was under construction. The

British Engineers traced the roadway (from Kandy) to link up with the existing Jaffna-Mullaitivu roadway at Yakkachchi - the sharp turn there reminds any one of it. To the Overseer (contractor) from Pt. Pedro who was doing the road construction, finding water was his problem. His labourers toiled hard in pushing the water-cart, all the way, to old Murikandy where some water remained even in the dry season. The task was arduous and the toil heavy and even in the Murikandy swamp, water was fast drying up. It was during one of those dejected nights that he dreamt of excavating a well, even though in solid granite, near the 151 mile post on the new roadway, but with little success in striking water. His enthusiasm waned and he was dejected and sad and in disturbed slumber, he received divine directions that he should first attend to the obsequies of a mendicant lying dead in the jungle at old Murikandy.

In the Vanni area, we often come across travelling mendicants who go from village to village; many of them are savants of very high religious attainment, who mingle with the people as they have to work out their (savants') karma. One such was known to visit old Murikandy village often. He carefully carried a special stone under his armpit wrapped in clothes. He would set up this stone, and after anointing it, perform his daily Vigneswara pujas to the stone. When at Murikandy, his usual stopping place for the night was, not the village itself, but in the jungle close by. This is not a frequented place and a corpse can lie there undetected for several days.

Moolasthanam at old Murikandy Temple, 1963
The Savant's Stone

The overseer and his gang, coming to old Murikandy found the mendicant's body and performed the customary obsequies and some sort of shed was erected to house the mendicant's stone. Then returning to their work site, blasted further the well at 151 M.P. and to their delight struck water which gushed up. The well served all their needs. It continues to do so, even to this day, catering for all the needs of the travellers who pass by up and down Jaffna-Kandy road. The Theru-murikandy (at 151 M.P.) commemorates the event and stands as a beacon symbol to the simple shrine erected at old Murikandy, installing the savant's precious stone, in the moolasthanam there.

We were shown the dilapidated cadjan shed shrine housing the sacred stone. Very soon a hat collecton served the wherewithal to effect immediate improvements and prevent it from falling down. Later, with improvements to the tank, the village was re-habilitated with more persons coming to reside in the village and working the fields. The shrine also benefited by getting a permanent structure that would not fall down. The villagers and we celebrated the Kumba-abishekam ceremonies on 23rd August, 1963.

The savant's stone, which presides as the Moolasthana Ganesha Moorthy of the temple at old Murikandy is shown in the picture, with abishekam ceremonies.

10. APPAL AHANRA ANAIMUGANIN ATPUTHAM, MURIKANDY

I was a frequent traveller on the Kandy-Jaffna road during the years 1949-50, as my residence was at Vavuniya. At the Murikandy stopping place, near the 151 M.P. there were only the thatched shrine, one well and one poor tagaram shed which served as a tea boutique run by one Arumugam. Those days there was not much road traffic. The well, which no doubt was the gift of the gods in years gone by, had like the legendary Annapoorani (or Bhahiravan), served the needs of the Murikandy shrine, the needs of the tea boutique, the labourers living in the labour lines, the travellers who stop for their ablutions (it was a notion of mine that many stopped there more for the water, washing and tea, than for dharshan of Vinayaka Moorthy) and on Fridays the devotees who come there for pongal ceremonies. The latter are generally late and have to eke out the drops that drain into the well sump.

Improvements and augmentation of the water resources of the area became a most urgent subject. Going on the usual saying that in the Vanni, a tank means a village and a village means a tank (and if the tank breaches the village migrates), we scanned the neighbourhood for any abandoned tank, the restoration of which would enable the building up of a village at Murikandy (near the 151 M.P.). Incidentally it would enable regular puja ceremonies at the shrine by boosting its income, without having to depend on contributions from passers by, which was seasonal.

Meanwhile it caused a great deal of pain of mind to Arumugam (of the boutique) to witness the unpleasant relationship between the management and the priest (poosari) of the shrine, who was often made the scapegoat for diminishing collections at the shrine. It was Arumugam's kind consolations that preserved peace. But he too was getting fed up. Very soon he went about saying that, in a dream, the god Vinayaka Moorthy had announced to him that He (Vinayakar) intended shifting from the place (appal ahanru poha).

Soon afterwards one day the railway labourers, during their return after work to their lines, noticed an **elephant trunk-like-growth** on the trunk of a palu tree about 500 yards south along the road, from the shrine. With Arumugam's regular fondling of the growth, annointing it and with pujas, the growth gradually did assume the shape of Ganesha Moorthy. I too paid obeisance to the growth in the tree and witnessed the puja, so did thousands of passers by. To all a miracle had happened. I used to watch with interest the talk and conversation amongst the travellers themselves on the subject. Very soon the palu tree, with the Ganesha growth, also became a regular halt and worship-place of the passers by and there were then two places to venerate (and to contribute) at Murikandy. Most people stopped at both the Pilliyar sites (they were only 500 yards apart). Those who were in a hurry stopped at one or at the other, but the more devoted ones, made a first stop at the new tree site and from there proceeded walking on foot for dahrshan of the Ganesha Moorthy of the shrine, treating that as the moolasthanam of an imagined large temple of which the tree carried the entrance (vasal) Pilliyar.

Our search for abandoned tanks in the locality, assumed actual action on New Year's Day of that year. Many volunteers from all ranks assembled at the shrine and after partaking of pongal offered by some devotees commenced following the trace of a streamlet flowing past a road culvert. The more vigorous among us cut jungle and hacked away to form a path while the others kept a look out for any mounds by the banks, which they had been advised by me, may be the indication of a tank-bund breach. The going was slow in the mid-day sun and cutting jungle was fatiguing and enthusiasm was beginning to wane; all of a sudden Kandiah (Head Clerk, being stout he led the path cutting gang) yelled snake!, snake!. There it was, a cobra all coiled up, right in Kandiah's path, on a mound; when it had been scared off, we found to our amazement that the snake-mound extended and gradually as we hacked away (furiously now) there came into view a breached tank bund. Clearing a path (with glee) along the top of the abandoned over grown bund, we got to its end and what a surprise awaited us! There it was, through the jungle growth we could see, we were coming up bang on the palu tree with Ganesha Moorthy growth on it. Emotional feelings overtook all of us and we lay at the foot of the tree; some cried, some rested, others slept. One embittered person whispered 'Pilliyar is often unfair. He could easily have directed us, in a dream or done something, instead of sitting and watching us cutting jungle, laboriously in this hot sun, before making this, which was His revelaton.'

Soon afterwards, steps were taken to restore the tank and a colonisation scheme was founded at the place, for the development of 32 acres of irrigated fields. That automatically founded a new settlement.

Consequently we now have several houses, shops, permanent buildings and what is more, several wells at Murikandy, over all of which Vinayakar is presiding majestically, and Arumugam is a contented colonist.

Postscript:

1. Ganesh no longer starves during rainy days.

2. The tree with the Ganesha growth was cut down along with other trees that were cut under 'removal of roadside shrines' scheme. But that 'avathar' had completed its purpose and there was no need for it to remain there any longer.

11. VIGNA VINAYAKAR TEMPLE, AKKARAYANKULAM, KILINOCHCHI

Sthalam-moorthy-theertham, had been an ancient auspicious combination. So it was of the ancient Vigna Vinayakar temple at Akkarayan-kulam Tank. The area had flourished during the Vanni regime when settlers colonised the Vanni areas, among whom such names as Akka Rayan, Pallava Rayan and Kanaga Rayan, have been handed down to posterity, as leaders.

Such temples would have suffered the ravages of loot and devastation as had been the fate of many Hindu Temple in the 16th Century,. A simple stone, with a few cadjans overhead however remained to posterity, on this tank bund. Akkarayankulam was known to have been in a breached and abandoned condition, says H. W. Parker who reported on it in 1904, and so said Capt. Schneider earlier in 1801.

Active interest in its restoraton commenced in 1949. At the time there was however no regular path to the site, other than those made by those who go hunting, to whom this area was a favourite haunt. Losing their way and with their transport getting bogged, our inspecting party found safe refuge on tree tops, and awaiting persons at Kilinochchi suffered heartache. That was in the year 1949.

The tank was subsequently restored in 1954, with that, the restoration of the Pilliyar temple, demolished for tank construction, was completed in 1961. To one's recollection, the names of S. Arumugam, A. Shivasunderam, N. Periyathamby and S. Maruthappu appear. However all credit for the restoration goes to S. Appiah but for whose enthusiasm the restoration would not have been completed.

Akkarayankulam Pillaiyar Temple - The Abisheka Procession 1961

The Kumba Abishekam ceremonies were held on 03 February1961. Pictures taken at the time may be seen. The temple and the Pilliyar were entrusted to the much devoted hands of one S. Thiraviam.

Due chiefly to the selfless service of Thiraviam, who had taken the maintenance of the temple as his life task, improvements were done in 1963 with the building of a Mandapam and also a separate madapaly structure by the side.

The allottees of lands under the right bank channel commenced taking an active interest subsequently and much credit goes to the President of the Multi-Purpose Co-operative Society, V. Swaminathan, for the very active interest taken in the temple. Due to his enthusiasm it became possible to erect a 'gem' of a Bell Tower in front and also new Vasantha Mandapam. He was also instrumental in getting composed an 'oonjal paaddu' - a garland of verses to be recited after puja time.

S. Thiraviam, though of ripe old age, still continues to serve Pillaiyar and maintain the temple in satisfactory function. Steps were being taken in 1979 to appoint a priest in charge.

Regular pujas and festivals are observed at the temple.

Kumba Abishekam,1961. S. Appiah is seen facing the camera

12. MULANGAVIL PILLAIYAR KOVIL, PUNAKARI

A half way halting place between Jaffna and Mannar along the coastline roadway is the hamlet of Mulangavil. Tradition attributes the formation of this Villu (or low ground) to natural cavern formation due to decomposition of the limestone; as its name would indicate this villu was formed without a thunderbolt puncturing the terrain.

However formed, the 'Villu' becomes a receptacle for storage of water and the hamlet Mulangavil is a landmark, as a watering place on the Jaffna-Mannar journey. A Government circuit bungalow (now in ruins) was erected here, for the convenience of the provincial administrative officers travelling to Mannar.

Old Pillaiyar Shrine Mulangavil, 1950 Size about 2ft by 2ft only

All passers-by pay their obeisance to a pillaiyar stone, installed conspicuously, perhaps by some travelling mendicant. For all the reverence paid to it, it was a mere stone, oval in shape. One wonders if it is the sole remnant of a once flourishing temple. I am unable to recollect its history which was told to me by the retired Udaiyar of Ponnaveli, a much respected person.

With the advent of the Thiruketheeswaram Era and the consequent upsurge in matters relating to Hindu temples, V. K. Chellappah Swamy was able to make temporary arrangements in 1951, for a person to be at the site and receive contributions for the building of a shrine. Very soon other persons took interest and accepted responsibility and the site developed, becoming a shrine. By 1961, collecting stones for a structure had been commenced. With the growth of land development projects in the vicinity there came more devotees and the foundation for a temple structure was ceremonially laid on 24th June 1964. The structure was completed and a Vigneshwara Moorthy (made by sculptors in India) was installed on 10th June 1965; among those who identified themselves in the undertaking were M. Sri Kantha (Govt. Agent), Jaffna the retired Udaiyar of Ponnavely, K. Arulamplam, and other residents of Punakari.

Pictures show the old wayside shrine and some of those who were present on Kumba-abishekam day, 10th June, 1965.

With the establishment of the Mulangavil Highland Colonisation project, the area is being rapidly developed. Many devotees gather at the Pillaiyar temple now at puja times.

New Mulangavil Pillaiyar Temple
Devotees on Kumba Abisheham day, of new Shrine 1965

It is also a convenient half-way halting place for the buses that travel from Mannar to Punakari en-route to Jaffna.

13. ATHIMODDAI PILLAIYAR KOVIL, ATHIMODDAI, MANNAR

Athimoddai village is reached by turning off right near the 19th mile on the Mannar-Punakari road, and proceeding about two or three miles.

When we first visited the place in 1963, it was a hamlet of a few thatched cottages but sporting a permanent school building and a temple. We learnt from the elders of the place that it was once a flourishing settlement, historically associated with the Thiruketheeswaram temple. Ancient brickwork in an abandoned well was shown to us. Rice cultivation was restricted to the few small minor tanks around, of which Illantaimoddai Kulam was the biggest. Due to insufficiency of water, successful cultivation was precarious and many villagers had abandoned the place.

At temple puja time, we worshipped Ganesha Moorthy, the sole vigraham in the dilapidated temple with broken walls and half open roof through which sunlight was streaking into the moolasthanam. Ponnambalam, an elderly villager, apologised for the dilapidated condition of the temple.

Mannar Athimoddai Vinayakar-1963 - Pooja time

Kurai tank a few miles higher up had been inspected by engineers several years earlier but adversely reported on, as building a tank by the side of the neighbouring major river Paranki aru was not a sound proposition. We wondered what the term 'Kurai' stood for. Did it actualy indicate the thorny kurai bush. Suddenly illumination came to us, that kurai could indicate a part or a portion of a reservoir. It all fitted in, as was confirmed later. A large major reservoir, a Perunkulam, had been constructed by damming the flow of the Paranki aru. This served to fill various starved minor tanks of the locality. With the breaching of Perunkulam (Kurai kulam and Kunchi kulam, remained) the minor tanks which depended on Perunkulam for supply, were starved and many were abandoned. So it was well worth restoring Kurai tank, as it was (for the immediate present), a first step to rebuilding the major Perunkulam reservoir. Steps were taken.

Many residents who had migrated returned to the village. The Temple also had been repaired and improved by 1965. The Athimoddai Pillaiyar now presides quite happily over His devotees, in a good temple structure,

Vinayakar's devotees assembled for temple restoration, 1965

14. KATHANKULAM PILLAIYAR TEMPLE, AND ANCIENT SANTHIRASEKARAN TEMPLE, CHEDDIKULAM

About fifteen miles from Madawachchy on the road to Mannar is a small, and not so well maintained, shrine dedicated to the worship of Vinayaka Moorthy. The site and the tank, across the road, known as Muhattan Kulam commemorates (Kattar) an ancient holy site, situated by Vavalai, about four miles interior to the South.

The Manual of the Vanni, by J. P. Lewis (1895) has the following: 'The Division of Cheddikulam is said to have been colonized in the Kaliyuga 3348 (about 247 A.D.) by a chetty from Madura, who with some Parava pearl fishers had been wrecked on the coast of Ceylon. This is the account given of it: Vira Narayana Cheddi came to Adankapattu, settled in Cheddikulam, built or dug the kerni called Vavalai, and erected a temple to Santhirasekeran. He buried in a well near the temple treasure which took sixty elephants to carry, and left a devil Chadamuni to watch over it, and local tradition has it that, this treasure will be revealed by the muni who is guarding it (Katan), to any one who rebuilds the temple that was destroyed by the Portuguese '. That was the end of ancient Santhirasekaran Temple of the Vanni regime at Cheddikulan.

But the temple cannot now be rebuilt at the original site near Vavalai Lake as that area will soon get submerged by the Malwattu Reservoir. So Kathankulam has been restored and the Muhakathankulam colony established with a Pillaiyar temple for worship.

It is still hoped, by those of us who worked hard for the speedy restoration of the work in 1950, that the treasure will be revealed to us, even modified, due to shifting the site of the temple to the road side and dedicating it to Vinayakar.

A priest is resident at the site and performs pujas. Attempts were being made in 1979 to re-build the temple facing the roadway

Reference:

Navaratnam C S 'A Short History of Hinduism', page 53

15. MAMANGA ISWARA PILLAIYAR TEMPLE, BATTICALOA

About two miles North of Batticaloa town are found the celebrated Mamanga Theertham, Amirthakali Theertham and the Hanuman Theertham, all in the vicinity of the Batticaloa Bar, where the fresh waters of the Batticaloa Lake flow into the ocean. The location had been a theertha karai from time immemorial. It is known as Amirthakali village. Amirtham is the unobtainable elixir of life and kali describes the soil. In this celebrated village is found the Mamanga Iswara Temple also known as Mamanga Pillaiyar temple with the sacred Siva Lingam in the sanctum.

Like many of the places of worship, in the eastern coastal region, Amirthakali also with its temple and its theerthams has legends associating it with Sri Rama Bhagavan, Hanuman, and Ravana the Emperor of Lankapuram. It is general tradition to ascribe many of the Siva Sthalams along the eastern coast as halting places of Ravana, on his journeys from Lankapura to Thiru Koneswaram, his favourite place of worship. Hanuman is said to have found solace here by extinguishing the burning flare of his tail by dipping it in the waters of what is now known as Hanuman Theertham. He himself was amazed at its value and performed pujas here. Devotees seek today the therapeutic value of the waters of the theertham where ancient rishies are said to have poured the sacred waters of the Ganges. Sri Rama is said to have rested here and performed obsequies to the many that departed in the Ramayanam battles, before returning to his home in Ayodia.

Whatever all these may be, we know that at one time the Batticaloa region was occupied by Vaddah folks. The story is that once a Veddah boy discovered a Lingam under a tree in the jungle and told his parents, who revered it by building a shrine around it. In evidence, we find today the 'Kumarathan Kovil' in the vicinity.

I had a talk with the management on the 15th July, 1971, when I went to make my obeisance to Mamangeswaran. The revelation was made how one of their ancestors came across a Siva Lingam in the Jungle. It was brought and installed here at this spot; it had always been a theertha sthalam, and as the devotees are traditionally used to having a Vinayakar by the theertha-karai, a silver canopy of Pillaiyar was therefore, placed over the Lingam. All this happened on Maha Mamangam day, which occurs only once in twelve years; the deity became to be known as Mamanga Iswara Pillaiyar and Mamangeswarar, for short. It is usual to associate temples for the worship of the Shiva Lingam in the eastern region with the reign of Maga in the thirteenth century. Strangely enough the name of this temple has not figured in the list of temples destroyed during the invasions by foreigners.

The Mamanga Temple of today is a place of worship for thousands of devotees.

It was last renovated in 1960. Located in an attractive setting of coconut groves, and vast open spaces, spotted with bathing places and madams for pilgrims to rest, devotees gather here seeking solace.

In the temple both Sivan and Pillaiyar festivals are observed. The annual festival is held in July and for the Adi-Amavasay (new moon day in July) whole of Batticaloa, and more are here. It is the climax of the festivals here. The Kurunta tree, held sacred for Lord Siva, for He holds discourses seated under it, continues to flourish here.

Reference:

Many compositious have been forthcoming on the Lord of Mamangam. They are the Mamanga Pathiham, Mamanga Unjal and Mamanga Kavadi Chinthu.

16. VEIYUL UKANDA PILLAIYAR TEMPLE, NALLUR, JAFFNA

Kulangai Singai Ariyan was the first Ariya Chakravarti King of Jaffna (13th century). When he built Nallur, his capital city, he sought divine protection to the celebrated city by erecting temples for worship of Hindu deities, in the four directions around it.

Veiyul Ukanda Pillaiyar Kovil was erected in the eastern approaches to Nallur. It is said that the structure of the temple was so devised that sunlight could penetrate into the innermost holy of holies.

Veiyul Ukanda Pillaiyar Temple, Nallur

The temple is believed to have been destroyed along with several other Hindu temples when the Kingdom of Jaffna fell into the hands of the Portuguese in 1621.

At Nayanmar Kaddu, Nallur, there is now a recent structure erected for the worship of Vinayaka Murthi. Ten day annual festivals are celebrated, finishing with the water cutting ceremony on 'panguny uththiram' day, in March-April.

17. KALVALAI PILLAIYAR TEMPLE SANDILIPAY, JAFFNA

In the heart of the Jaffna Peninsula is Sandilipay, consisting of two villages, Nadu Kuruchchi and the pristine Kalvalai. Kalvalai, as its name would indicate is a round rocky spur and may have been the ancient name for the present Sandilipay. Here is found a simple shrine to Katpaha Vinayakar said to have originated when a Pillaiyar - like stone was found while excavating. Kalvalai Pillaiyar has been immortalised in history, by an 'Anthathy' or song offering, composed by Sinnathamby Pulavar, a well known poet who lived in Nallur, Jaffna about 200 years ago, during the regime of the Dutch.

His father, Villavaraya Mudaliyar, was a highly respected person of Nallur. Due to his learning and noble deeds, he occupied a high position and was commissioned by the Dutch Government to chair a committee of twelve eminent persons to draft the 'Thesavalamai', the law concerning the 'customs and laws of the Tamils of Jaffna'. This is known to have been completed by April 1707.

Young Sinnathamby, who failed as a youth, however gained eminence as he grew up and won the favour and respect of Ganesa Iyer, a distinguished literary person of the period.

Kalvalal Pillaiyar Kovil, Sandilipay
Extolled by Sinnathamby Pulavar, a 17th century Nallur poet, the Kovil is a sacred heritage of the people.

Besides the Kalvalai Anthathi, in praise of Katpaha Pillaiyar, reigning at the Kalvalai Pillaiyar Kovil, Sinathamby Pulavar is known to have composed 'Marai sai An-thathy' dedicated to the Iswara deity at Vethamiyam, 'Parallai Vinayakar Pallu' extolling

Vinayaka Murthi at Parallai, Chulipuram and 'Katavai Velan Kovai' concerning an individual named Velauthampillai.

An 'anthathy' is a form of poetic composition in which each verse commences with the word at the end of the previous verse. The 'antham' provides the cue for the 'athi' of the next. It is usually used in composing garlands of verses in praise of a divine.

In the Kalvalai Anthathy the poet describes how Katpaha Vinayaka Murthi is majestically installed at Kalvalai, amidst groves of trees and 'thallai' in which are found conches. He says that Vinayakar is revered by celestial dwellers of the three worlds. The reader is besought to worship the Murthi and prostrate before him, if he is to be freed from his Karma, all of unlimited poetic vision and countless praises extolling the deity.

We do not of course find anything so impressive when we go to the temple today. A simple temple structure is seen; besides the sanctum there is a recently renovated shrine to Bhairava. Two priests officiate alternatively each year. Near the entrance is an ancient shrine to Naga Thambiran, where an annual Pongal ceremony is celebrated.

A local committee is engaged in the administration and in making arrangements for the rituals and ceremonies held in the temple.

Reference:

Nallur Sinnathamby Pulavar, 'Kalvallai Anthathy' (Tamil), published by the Saiva Paripalana Sabai, Jaffna, 1934.

18. OMANTAI PILLAIYAR TEMPLE, VAVUNIYA

Ten miles north of Vavuniya, on the road to Jaffna, is the celebrated ancient village of Omantai. What connection it had with ancient Mantai, directly opposite on the western coast, it has not been possible to trace; it could have been the eastern boundary of Mantai's territorial region; some say that it is its eastern reflection and that is O-Mantai. Others say that Omantai is just colloquial for 'KO-Manthai' meaning grazing grounds for cows. Being thirty miles away from Murihandi, in the north, it had always been a convenient resting place for Vinayaka's devotees.

Historically, Omantai had been very much in the foreground, when it was the seat of one of the Vanni chieftains during the Vanniyar regimes. We read of its chieftain being decorated in Mudaliyar Rasanayagam's 'Ancient Jaffna'. Nayaratnam endorses with (ref 1):- 'Omantai was once the head quarters of the Vanni Chiefs. There is a stone Saivaite Temple of the Vanniya times. Close to this Village Mara-Illupai possesses a ruined Saivaite temple.'

Omantai Pillaiyar Temple, Vavuniya
A permanent building has since been erected

It is said that it was one of the stopping places of the procession conveying the sacred Bo-tree sapling to Anuradhapura, enroute from Jambukovalam, the northern ancient sea port.

In this celebrated village was the Pillaiyar temple which was a cadjan shed in the year 1948; situated right by the roadside, passers-by stop and make their obeisance and also rest a while. Very likely the Pillaiyar temple may have been originally on the embankment of a tank. But that tank is no more, due to subsequent development, with the road and rail road going through it.

Whatever all that may have been, to me, the problem, in the year 1949, was the rebuilding of the tank at Omantai, that extends along the road going westward, which had been lying breached and abandoned for centuries.

Many of the village folks also had therefore migrated. We were undeterred by an advance entry in the files dissuading any attempt at restoration due to railway cutting across. In our enthusiasm **anything was possible, if Pillaiyar would will it so**. So, a pongal at the pillaiyar temple was arranged and our womenfolk started making a hundred mothahams, while we proceeded with paraphernalia. Even as we surveyed and took levels, we felt the mothaham taking effect for the railroad and the railroad embankment was up higher and higher. The result was - Lo! The project was found to be feasible and all of us, Pillaiyar, the village folks, our womenfolk and us enjoyed the pongal.

At the home-front that night, in order to preserve marital harmony and domestic peace, I did agree with my wife that for every 'Mothagam' that was prepared, the railway embankment went up an inch. There were of course, others who would not assign that credit to Pillaiyar's ability but realistically attributed it to our faith and effort in entering into the muck and slosh of the tank bed under the bridge to obtain correct levels and not merely decide feasibility by a glance from a distance; the tall grass in the water can easily cause erroneous perceptions.

However it may have been, the embankments were found high enough to permit restoration of the tank.

The tank was restored and the settlement rehabilitated. The temple has also been rebuilt with a proper masonry walled building. A flourishing village is there now with its ancestral traditions.

Reference:

1.   Navaratnam, C.S., 'Vanni and the Vanniyas', 1960, page 10

19. BALA VINAYAKAR TEMPLE, CAPTAIN'S GARDENS, COLOMBO

During the days of the Dutch regime, in this Island, there was a little islet called 'Meththuwa' in the delta of the Kelani Ganga at Colombo. This Meththuwa very soon became a base for the receipt of local produce of spices and cinnamon transported by boats down the river from the hinterland, Avissawela.

There was a chief organiser for all this trade and merchandise, who calling himself 'Captain', received the goods and kept them for shipment when the Dutch ocean going vessels called at the port of Colombo. He had quite a large gathering of an Indian chetty community called 'Thiruvilanga Nagarathar', who were associated with him in this mercantile undertaking. In the course of time with the departure of the Dutch all this dwindled off.

However during the heyday of life of the nagarathars or chettiars in the island, they had commenced here a Vinayaka shrine, for their religious observances. It is believed that was about the year 1702. Mention is also made in this connection of an important personage, of the time, an interpreter of the Malayalam language, who had assumed the name of Francis Paulus Sooriyamoorthy. However religious matters became definite and well pronounced, when in 1817 one Sivan Poothapar donated 5 1/2 acres of land for the Vinayakar temple.

During those years, a Chettiyar devotee of the Vinayaka deity who was bereft of any offspring made a vow; his vow was that he would erect a proper Sivan temple to house the Siva Linga Murthi that was then languishing in the open, under a tree in the garden. In course of time he was blessed with a son. In fullfilment of his vow he erected Kailasa Natha Sivan Kovil by the side and named his son Kailasa Nathar. One can therefore well appreciate the then-cherised belief among the newly weds that Pillaiyar's tharisanam (worship) assures them a male offspring. But of course, it is not every couple who built a Sivan Kovil thereafter.

Whatever all that may be, these two temples in Captain's Garden, Colombo were gradually improved subsequently and became land marks for Hindu worship in the heart of the city. The Sivan temple was improved and comprehensively built up later in 1933.

In 1931 a proper Trustee Board took charge and has improved the small Vinayaka temple vastly. No story of the growth of this temple is complete without the mention of the name of B. Shanmuganatha Sarma Kurukkal, chief priest, whose service and continuous effort brought 'Captain's Garden Pillaiyar Temple', to become a most prominent temple in the city of Colombo.

Today we have in the temple, besides the two centuries old Vinayaka deity in the sanctum, a Sanmuga Murthi Vigrakam and a Lakshmi Devi deity installed in their niches, on either side of Ganesa deity. The many utsava and other murthies are on a platform facing south. The long mandapam terminates with a small high Bhairava shrine. At the entrance a magnificent seven tiered Raja Gopuram, 67 ft high is being erected. This would provide an imposing sight to the Vinayaka temple.

Great credit is to be given to the Managing Trustee Board, who have laboured hard for this Vinayaka Devasthanam. Regular pujas are performed daily. All Hindu festivals are observed with great care. The annual festivals draw large crowds of devotees. The temple enjoys the patronage of eminent citizens of Colombo.

20. RUINS OF MEDIEVAL VINAYAKAR TEMPLES

Impressive gems of architecture and sculpture are to be seen in the ruins of Hindu temples of the 10th and 11th centuries in Polannaruva. These are remnants of temples built during the era of the Chola regime. Jana Natha Mangalam was their capital city. These temples are found in about eight groups and in each there had invariably been a shrine for Lord Vinayakar. At some of them the statue of Vinayaka Murthi has also been unearthed. Excavation work which was commenced during the years 1901-1905 is still being continued by the Archaeological Department.

The Vinayaka Shrines had generally been much smaller than the main temple of the group. But these too have been erected in keeping with traditional requirements. In some, the shrine consists of a garbagrakam and a mandapam. Others are just one roomed shrines. Only the bases are to be seen today at each shrine; these are of granite stone or of brickwork. There is no superstructure at any of these in existence now.

Some of the Vinayaka shrine ruins are described below. Detail reports may be seen in the Annual Reports of Archaeological Commissioner, published as Govt. Sessional Papers.

At the Northern Gate but within the walls of the Ancient City are found the ruins of three temples each different from the other in form and structure, dedicated to three foremost deities of the Hindu Pantheon.

The somewhat unusual type of structure what had existed at the West side of the city gate had evidently housed Vinayaka Murthi as a beautifully sculptured statue of Vinayaka mounted on mooshikam rat, had been found in the ruins of the shrine. Only the traces of the building are discernable now: it evidently consisted of an inner garbagrakam, and a long mandapam.

The pedestal or asanam at the moolasthanam (sanctum) and the Komukam outlet to the north are among the finds during the excavation of the structure, in 1908; these are found at the site today.

The Vinayaka shrine found among the ruins of the temple on the Anavulandawa Road, (Siva Devale No. 5) had been of brickwork. It had consisted of the traditional layout of an inner garbagrakam and an outer mandapam.

The Vinayaka shrine found at the temple built in memory of the Chola Queen Vanavan Mahadevi (Siva Devale No. 2) had been a square only. A well carved slab sculpture of Vinayaka Murthi was found here.

There had been a Vinayaka shrine of the elaborate Pandyan architectural type temple. Buried in the ruins here was found a statue of Vinayaka Murthi. A special feature in it is the mooshikam (Lord Ganesa's Vahanam), depicted running up the asanam of the heavily seated deity.

The bronze icons found in the ruins of these Hindu temples are examples of superb gems of art and sculpture. In fact some of them have been declared, by eminent persons, as best ever found, superior even to those found in India.

The bronze Vinayaka Murthi unearthed in the 1960 excavations, (at Siva Devale No. 5) is an example of a large but nevertheless exquisitely beautiful work of art. The back view reveals the intricate high standard of workmanship attained by the artist.

In the Vanni Districts

Vinayaka is the special deity of the Vanni agricultural folks. He is the guardian of their crops. Ruins of a Vinayaka shrine or at least a representing stone may be found at every tank bund, sometimes at the edge of paddy fields too; Vinayaka places of worship are found everywhere in the Vanni districts, in fact as you enter the Vanni, you feel His presence and his watchful eye. A simple devout breaking of a coconut, would humour him.

At Kotta Kerni, northwest of Kokkulai lagoon, South of Mullaitivu, the Archaeogical Commissioner records in his Annual Report for the year 1905, finding 'a lonely temple ... with an oily smooth-blackened image, of Ganesa in a little palm leaf hut-is all the Temple. But it seems a place of pilgrimage for the villagers from miles around.'

Reference:

Annual Reports of the Archaelogical Commissioner published as Sessional Papers - 1901.

SECTION II

SIVAN KOVILS

21. VENERATION OF SIVA

The Supreme One is venerated as Lord Siva by the Saivaite Hindus. The Vedic eras saw Rudra venerated as a powerful Divine lord of sacrifices, god of storms etc, who granted prosperity and welfare. His more abstract and peaceful Form becomes venerated as the transcendental God Lord Siva. Siva along with Brahma and Vishnu form the 'Holy Trinity' of the Hindu Pantheon, responsible for creation, preservation and destruction.

Many Aspects and Names

As Supreme Lord of the Universe, Siva is conceived in several Forms; each of these bears a separate name having its aspects represented by an image or symbol. 'Maha Deva' enthrones him Supreme, worshipped even by the Celestial Devas. 'Iswara' extols his overall Lordship, 'Maheswara' his Lordship of Knowledge, 'Sankara' his Lordship and giver of Joy. He is 'Santhira-sekaran as he wears the Crescent Moon in his braid, 'Dhakshana Murthi' when seated in meditation facing the South, and 'Pasupathi' when acting as the Divine Herdsman. He is 'Maha Linga Murthi' when represented by the Linga symbol, and as 'Lord Nadarajah' he is the King of the Dance Divine.

Siva Lingam

The Siva Lingam installed and presiding in the sanctum of all Sivan Temples is the Symbol of Lord Siva. It is a mystic symbol of Vedic origin representing that which is formless and has been the object of veneration for ages. The Parasurameswara Lingam, the earliest known Hindu deity, believed to be of the 1st or 2nd centuries is still extant today at Gaudamallam.

Physically the Lingam is an assembly of three componant parts. The seating Avudaiyar consist of a Brahma Paham and a Vishnu Paham slabs. These interlock with a cylindrical Rudra Paham which stands upright symbolically reaching the sky and around which the whole universe revolves.

Hindu mythology associates the five elements of the ancient world, each with a Siva Lingam to be venerated at five celebrated Siva Sthalams in India, as follows: water (appu) at Kasi Jambukeswaram, fire (Theivu) at Arunachchalam Thiru-Annamalai, air (vaivu) at Kalahasti, earth (piruthivi) at Kanchi, and space (akasa) at Chidamparam.

To facilitate veneration by devotees at one location, five small Lingams are assembled symbolically and are installed in one shrine in the Southern Prahara of Sivan Temples.

Ananda Nadarajah

Nadarajah is the Dance Form of Lord Siva. It is a form of exquisite beauty which has won high acclaim of the whole world. This form was revealed to sages after long periods of meditation and is said to depict Lord Siva dancing at Holy Chidambaram, symbolic of the inner hearts of mankind.

In this Form, Siva stands in a circle of flame. His upper arms bear a drum and fire representing sound (vibration) and light. The two lower are in the abhaya (fear not) and seek refuge poses. His braided locks carry Ganga and the Crescent moon. The crushing of all evil forces is depicted by the Asura lying crushed under the Lord's foot.

The Form depicts rhythm and perpetual movement of energy in the universe, declared by modern scientists, as atoms in motion causing constant vibration. The Form thus symbolises cosmic activity of which Lord Siva is the activist Director or the King of the Dance.

Anthropomorphic Representation

Siva is sometimes depicted in anthropomorphic or almost human-like Form. In this he is seen as an ascetic, with body smeared with ash and wearing a garland of human skulls. A tiger's skin is thrown over his shoulders and a snake encircles his neck. Armlets of bones are also seen. The two upper arms bear the Trident and the axe, while the two lower are in the familiar abhaya boons giving pose. Various interpretations have been given for this Form.

Puranas and Saiva Saints

The Puranas extol Lord Siva's Grace to his devotees. Many are the incidents narrated in them of the Lord's intervention in human affairs. Supernatural intervention has come to the rescue of many a devotee from severe predicament. For all these, 'Faith' in him, has been the keynote. Many devotees went about in the middle ages, singing songs and dancing in ecstacy. Tradition has chosen sixty three of them who are today known as 'Nayanmars'. Of these, four who have outpoured with garlands of verses in his praise are outstanding. Their verses are recited today at every ceremony of the Hindus in the home and at the temple.

Worship

The most auspicious occasion for the worship of Lord Siva is the Sivarathri night in February-March. On this night is recited how Siva revealed himself from a Lingam in a flame of light. Other special occasions are the 'Prathosha' days twice every month. In general all Mondays of the week are auspicious for reverence to Siva Murthi;

Sivaya Namaha Aum
Siva Siva
Sivaya Namaha Aum!

Sivan Temples

Temples for veneration of Lord Siva are not many. They require strict adherence to agamic principles and so are not so readily undertaken. Most of them are found in the Jaffna Peninsula due chiefly to Arumuga Navalar's exhortation, about a hundred years ago. There are only a few in the Batticaloa District; in Trincomalee there are several ancient temples in ruins, besides the two now in function in the Town itself. In all about 25 Eswaran temples and another 25 Sivan temples could be identified; the total cannot be expected to exceed about a hundred.

In the pages that follow, in the rest of this Section, are described some Sivan Temples.

22. VAITHEESWARA-SIVAN KOVIL, VANNARPANNAI, JAFFNA

Also known as Chettiyar Shivan Kovil or Sivan Kovil, Vannarpannai, it is situated in Jaffna Town, on the Kankesanturai Road.

Vaithilinga Chettiyar, son of Gopala Chettiyar, built this temple, obtaining special permission granted by the Dutch rulers of Ceylon, in the year 1791. This is one of the few instances, where the Dutch Government eased their tolerance to other religions, a feature noticeable during the latter part of their regime, which lasted from 1658 to 1796 AC.

We read in page 110 of A. Mootootamby Pillay's 'Jaffna History', that Vaithilinga Chettiyar, a leading merchant, and one who enjoyed great influence with the Government, obtained the release of Nalla Mappana Vanniyan, Chief of Panakamam. The Vanniyan had been held by the Government for treason. Chettiyar obtained his release and paid the necessary ransom money of 1200 rix dollars.

Later Vanniyan showed his appreciation of Chettiyar's generosity by donating to the temple that Chettiyar was building, 20,000 palmyrah trees for timber. Further, in grateful obeisance to Vaitheeswara Moorthy and Thaiyal Nayaki Ambal, also worshipped as Valambikai Ambal, the incumbent deities of the temple, he donated Terangkandal, a village in Thunukai with its tank and paddy fields, income from which would assure the daily rituals and the performance of the pujas for the moorthies.

The Chettiyar had undoubtedly been advised by well-informed personages in temple construction. We find it complete with all traditional requirements of a Sivan Kovil. The inner praharam is replete with parivara moorthy temples. The Vasantha Mandapam was recently renovated and a Raja Gopuram is now under erection at the main entrance. The temple is well endowed.

Regular puja ceremonies and other Sivan Kovil festivals are conducted in good manner. Two annual festivals are held. The Sivan festivals last tor twenty days terminating with the full moon day in March and the Ambal Devi festivals last for ten days finishing with theertham on the new moon day in July.

23. SADDANATHAR KOVIL, NALLUR, JAFFNA

This temple was erected by Singai Ariyan (Kulangai) the first Ariya Chakravarti King of Jaffna: he built Nallur, his capital City, and sought divine protection to the celebrated city by the erection of Saddanathar Kovil to the North, Kailaya Nathar Kovil to the South, Veiyul Ukanda Pillaiyar Temple to the East and Veera Maha Kali Ambal Kovil to the West of Nallur. These temples were well maintained; by the succeeding Kings of Jaffna, notably Kanaka Suriya Singai Ariyan (1440-1478).

Saddanathar Kovil, Nallur

History has recorded the demolition of the temple, along with several others in the year 1621, when the Kingdom of Jaffna was taken over by Philip de Oliveira, the Portuguese Governor. Kalai Pulaver K. Navaratnam in his 'Tamil Element in Ceylon Culture' has mentioned the incident of the priests of the temple depositing the temple vikrahams in the neighbouring pond, before the temple was destroyed.

Early in the nineteenth century (about 1815) when there was a revival of Hinduism in the Island, one Thambaiyahpillai felt the divine urge to revive this temple. Excavating the Thirukulam (pond), some of the vigrakams of old were discovered. The Nallai Nayaki Ambal Vigraham which was found intact and which had special sculptural features and craftsmanship was accepted for re-installation and the inner temple was built with Linga Moorthy in the Moolasthanam. The other statues that were unearthed have been handed over to the Jaffna museum where they can be seen today. They include a Gajalakshmi, Thakshana Moorthy, Valli Deivayani and

Subramaniyar on a peacock carved from one stone, a Saneeswaran statue. These have been identified as belonging to the Vijayanagara period by Shanmuganathan, Assistant Conservationsist.

The temple was improved later by the progeny of the revivalist, Shivapragasapillai, who added the prahara moorthy temples and other structures needed in a Sivan temple. Later, Thambyahpillai built the Bell Tower, and carried out other restoration work of the old structures. Dr. T. Nallainathan installed a Pancha Linga Murthi of five Seiumbu Lingams taken from Narbada River, which bear distinguishing Charka markings. Abishekams and pujas are performed to these. Nalla Nayaki Ambal Sametha Nallai Natha Linga Moorthy presides at the Nallur Saddanathar Kovil for tharisanam by the many devotees who worship there. All the pujas and festivals which are usually held at Sivan temples are observed here.

24. KANNALINGESWARA SWAMY KOVIL, VADDUKODDAI WEST, JAFFNA

On the road to Moolai from Vaddukoddai is the Kannakambiga Smetha Kannalingeswara Swamy Kovil, often referred to locally as Kannagai Amman Kovil. The sacred Linga Moorthy is installed in the main sanctum, so that it is a Sivan Temple but with Kannagai Ambal Vigraham installed in the Shrine facing south.

Kanna Lingeswaram Temple Vaddukoddai

It is said locally that this temple was erected by a Brahmin named Ramanatha Paddar, who came from India, during the days of the Ariya Chakravarthy Kings of Jaffna. It is believed to have been built later as a proper temple and customary pujas established during the days of Sri Vengadesa Kurukkal in the year 1513. It may have been principally a Kannakai Ambal Kovil, then. We hear that it escaped demolition by the foreign invaders of the seventeenth century, as the raiding party was told that it was a 'Matha Temple', referring to the Pattini Devi enshrined in it. This name survives even to this day.

Kanna Lingeswara Moorthy

With the renaissance of Hinduism in the Navalar era, this temple which was then in a dilapidated state, was rebuilt and Kumba Abishekam performed, in 1882, by Tamil Scholar Sri N. Sivasubramaniya Sivachariar. The structure then assumed the pattern of a proper agamic Sivan Kovil with the Siva Lingam enshrined in it. Regular pujas and festivals commenced to be performed by the Sivachariar and his progeny thereafter.

The temple continued its function though on a diminishing note, as years passed, with support from Hindu residents in Malaya.

Kannakambigai Ambal

A Temple Restoraton Board, formed in 1975 took charge of its affairs and renovated the entire structure and a Maha Kumba Abishekam was performed on 12th July, 1978.

Kannakai Amman

Today we see in the temple the venerable P. Kurumoorthy Kurukkal of ripe old age, continuing to attend to its functions, from many many years ago. In the prahara are the Vinayaka and other shrines. A therppai-kulam adorns the temple.

The annual festivals are held in June.

25. KARAI NAGAR SIVAN KOVIL, EELATHU CHIDAMPARAM, JAFFNA

A Sivan temple situated at Karai Nagar, North-West of the Jaffna Peninsula has gained prominence as Elathu Chidamparam. It has been built at the site of an ancient Aiyanar temple at Thinnapuram, in Valanthalai, Karai Nagar.

We read, that in the era of the Tamil Kings, and the Vanni regime, one Muthu Manicam Chettiyar erected a temple for the worship of Aiyanar, at Viya, a neighbouring village, and held its inauguration - Kumba Abishekam ceremonies on the 25th day of the month of May in the year 1518. The temple was well built and richly endowed, so much so that it attracted the cupidity of the foreign invaders. The Portuguese who went to loot and plunder it in the year 1618 were thwarted by divine Grace but the Hollanders razed it to the ground subsequently in 1658.

Sivan Kovil, Karainagar, 1980

About two hundred years later, with the resuscitation of Hinduism in the Navalar era, one Andi Murugar received the Divine Urge for rebuilding the temple for Aiyanar.

He had nothing to go by regarding the old temple. So he sat himself under a banyan tree with a soolam (trident) and worshipped it as Aiyanar, awaiting a revelation. On receiving sacred guidance, he recovered the old Aiyanar Vigraham, which had been hidden in a low marsh, when the temple was demolished. Great was his joy and this was broadcast wide in the locality. To him came Ambalavi Murugar, who was to become his celebrated disciple. Between them sufficient funds were collected and a humble temple for Aiyanar was erected at Thinnapuram, where the Vigraham was discovered.

In due course, as years went by, Ambalavi Murugar, now the sole surviving founder, with his enthusiasm and religious zeal, made the Aiyanar temple a landmark for worship by the devotees of the place. He observed the festivals and practises adopted at Thillai (Chidamparam). Lord Siva revealed Himself to him through Aiyanar. He embarked with jubilation on building a Sivan Temple at the site. With great success he obtained the Moolasthana Moorthies sculptured at Chidamparam itself and the Karainagar Sivan Kovil that we see today was inaugurated in the year 1848.

The Tree

Here reigns Saunderambihai Ambal Smetha Sunderasa Moorthy for tharisanam by the thousands of devotees who gather. Since then several improvements and additions have been made and rededication Kumba-Abishekam ceremonies performed in the years 1903, 1934, 1950 and in 1970.

Besides the prahara moorthies of a Sivan temple, special place is given to the Aiyanar (of old) in a shrine parallel to the sanctum.

In the outer prahara stands the celebrated tree under which Thiru Murugar sat. A manika-madam provides accommodation for pilgrims. To the north of the temple is an Ashramam erected by Thangammal, widow of the well known lawyer Nadarajah. Here, recital of thevarams, puranam reading and bajanai singing are held regularly.

The annual festival at the temple is held for ten days in March/April. The most notable event is the festival in December, culminating with the ratham and the celebrated arthira abishekam and Tharisanam on Thiruvathirai day, when all Jaffna gather at Thinnapuram for tharisanam of the Divine Dance, as at Thillai Chidamparam.

In the illustration can be seen arrangements being made for building a proper Gopura Vasal Entrance to the temple, which work is being proceeded with vigorously.

Reference:

A monumental Puranam has been published, in Tamil, entitled 'Eelathu Chidamparam'. An abridged version is also available.

26. VARI VANA NATHA SIVAN KOVIL, CHAVAKACHCHERI
(THAN THONRIYA VARI VANA SIVA ALAYAM)

Near the railway station at Chavakachcheri is an ancient Sivan Temple called the 'Than Thonriya Vari Vana Siva Alayam', also referred to locally as 'Iththi Maraththady Sivan Kovil'. It is to be found adjoining a much bigger and newer Sivan Kovil dedicated to Lord Sandiresekaran.

The origin of the Than Thonriya Vari Vana Nathar is a delightful simple legend and is narrated in the 14th chapter of the Dakshana Kailasa Puranam. There lived in Thirvanji, in Chola Nadu, a generous merchant by the name of Virupaakhan. His name was well known as one who always feeds and donates gifts to mendicants and the needy. Lord Parameswara, who wanted to test him, came to him one day as a mendicant and asked for all his wealth and his possessions, which he readily gave; he then migrated to Lanka with his wife Visalachchi, took residence close to Kodikamam and decided to make a new living as a milk vendor. To his dismay, he found that whenever he passed a certain specific spot his milk pot would spill over or the pot would slip and fall spilling the milk. He narrated this to others and when they examined the ground at the spot, they discerned a most majestic Shiva Lingam. Very soon a Sivan Kovil was built in this 'Vanam of Varibushes' and 'Vari Vana Nathar' reigned supreme, relishing the daily abishekam with milk provided by Virupaakham, who lived happily thereafter.

Vari Vana Natha Sivan Kovi,l Chavakachcheri

Unfortunately we cannot see today the splendour of the Vari Appar Kovil, erected during the Chola era as tragedy fell to all Hindu temples when they were demolished by foreign invaders in the seventeenth century. In many of the temples the priests safeguarded the moolasthana vigrakams by immersing them in the theertha well or kerni.

The present temple that we see now at the site is of recent origin. There is a large beautiful therppaikulam. While this was being excavated, a big flood occurred and covered the whole terrain. As the flood waters subsided the walls of the neighbouring well collapsed and the well emptied itself revealing a majestic Chola Linga moorthy. Further excavations soon revealed the Sivakami Ambal Vigrakam and the Nandi Devar. All these are installed in the temple and bestow tharisanam to the many devotees, who worship at the 'Iththiadi Sivan Kovil'.

The temple is not very pretentious and no grand festivals are held. But regular pujas are performed daily and Vari Vana Nathar gets His daily abishekam, without having cause to spill or break any person's milk pot.

Vari Vana Nathar

Sivakami Ambal

Nanthi Devar

27. VAVUNIKULAM SIVAN TEMPLE, TUNUKKAI,
(ANCIENT SIVAN KOVIL BELOW VAVUNIKULAM RESERVOIR, IN RUINS)

Vavunikulam is an ancient irrigation reservior, situated about 8 miles South-West of Mankulam. It had been lying breached and abandoned for centuries but has since been restored, about 20 years ago.

As far back as 1868, the well known Engineer-Historian Henry Parker had visited the work and reported that 'it was in existence before the time of Duttha-Gamini and this may carry its construction back to the third century B.C .....' and that 'the raising of such an embankment as that of Vavunikulam would necessitate the presence of many hundreds of labourers accustomed to earth work; the amount of work done itself indicates that there was already a resident population in the District'.

Broken parts of Siva Lingams and temple structure, 1953

Pali Nagaram the celebrated city below Peli Wavi, which was the ancient name of Vavunikulam, had its place of worship. In the area known as Kovil Kadu, about half-a-mile below the reservoir embankment are found the foundations in ruins, of a Sivan Temple. Broken statues and temple equipment litter the site. Picture shows a Siva Lingam assembly found lying in parts.

Here then was the ancient Peli Wavi and Pali Nagaram of the pre-Christian period, enjoying pristine power and prestige with satellite suburbs of Manner Kulam, Paner Kulam, and Vaner Kulam.

After the Peli Wavi era of old, centuries later, we have the period of the Vanni regime, when the neighbouring Panankamam gains the foremost place. A Sivan temple that had been at the Kovil Kadu site had suffered at the hands of the foreigners ; the breaking into two of the statues and the Lingams of the medieval period, found at the site, can be seen in the picture. The contrast in workmanship between the Avudaiyar and the portion of the upright is readily discernable.

Today the Vavunikulam irrigation reservior has been restored and the area rehabilitated; the colonists are reviving much of the ancient lore of the once celebrated city. A temple has been erected in Kovil Kadu and a Vinayaka Moorthy installed; there is much enthusiasm and activity in the area.

Little did I realise that all this will be set in motion, when I first attempted to locate the ruins of this celebrated Wavi in 1949, then lying abandoned in thick animal infested jungle; anyhow thanks to tracker Kandiah who was the only one able to guide me into this jungle. He was a much disappointed man, at the end of the day, as he was debarred from shooting any, inspite of the many herds of deer and cheetahs that crossed our track. Very soon necessary steps were taken for the restoration works and much credit goes to Engineers N. Periyathamby and P. Muthiah who did the work and expedited the rehabilitation of the area.

Recent Work

The temple for Vinayakar has been erected near the site of the ruins of the ancient Sivan temple. Much enthusiasm has been shown by the colonists of the scheme regarding the upkeep of the new temple. The enthusiastic Sivan Temple Restoration Society is taking steps to erect a new Sivan Temple at the site.

Reference:

Parker, Henry W. in Govt. Sessional Papers XLVIII of 1886

28. PANANKAMAM SIVAN KOVIL, PANANKAMAM, MANKULAM

In the hinterland of the Northern Vanni, there exists a little hamlet of regal antiquity, known as Panankamam. The half dozen semi-thatched houses, though only a settlement in appearance, mark today, the abode where kings dwelt once.

The village of Panankamam is reached from Mankulam, turning off from the Tunukai road and proceedings past Vavunikulam, a distance of 15 miles. My visit to the place was with a view to effecting improvements and providing augmentation to this village tank, which was the source of plenty and the envy of the neighbouring villages. This tank stored rainfall to irrigate over 200 acres; annually several parties from the villages around proceed thither to partake in the successful cultivation. Truly this is one which should be improved, especially as the neighbouring Vavunikulam (Pali vavi of old) would definitely be restored one day. These were my thoughts then.

The chief citizen of the village, a mature person and a retired headman introduces with pride, the seven ancient wells found around the village in the jungle, the only permanent landmarks of the one time city that was, and we talk about the history of the village.

Panankamaan Sivam Kovil
Abishekam ceremony procession in 1970

Panankaman occupied a pre-eminent place during the regime of the Vanniyars, for it was the seat of the foremost of the Vanni Chieftans; it was the largest and most important of the principalities of the Vanni. Its outstanding figure, Kailaiya Vanniyan (1644-1678), resisted the Portuguese and the Hollanders. So Panankamam was not ravaged by the Portuguese, unlike other Vanni kingdoms, prior to 1658. However the Hollanders subdued Panankamam later during the time of Kailaiya Vanniyan's successor Nalla-Mappana Vanniyan, who brought fame to his Vanni Kingdom by being arrested for treason. He was released several years later.

The priceless possession of this ancient village is their Sivan Kovil, situated about a mile away in the jungle.

Inside the small 'garbagraha' of this pretty little temple presides the moolasthana Siva Linga Moorthy. The Gnana Devar Vinayaka Moorthy is housed in a suitable attic at the entrance. Three other small Lingams are found housed in small attics in the prahara veedy. These together with Nanthi Devar and palipeedam, complete this jungle shrine.

With the development work going all around, new life has come to this ancient village - Panankamam (Paner - Kamam) of old. New houses have come up.

In the picture may be seen an abishekam ceremony in procession (1970), the Siva Lingam and three Siva Thondar, who along with others are responsible for the maintenance of the temple and the performance of the daily pujas and other ceremonies.

The ancient mulasthana Siva Linga moorthy now installed

Three devoted Siva Thondar who were prominent, 1970

29. THAN THONRIYA ISWARAN TEMPLE, ODDICHUDDAN, MULLAITIVU

'If as tradition says a Lingam had appeared, we should realise that in this era, Lingams do not just appear by themselves; there must have been a temple and if there had been a temple, there would have been a village and for that to exist there must have been a tank of the size that could adequately serve the development of such a place', - that was what I said to a group of elders of the place, assembled at my request at the chief's office at Oddichuddan, on a Saturday afternoon several years ago. We were on a quest to locate the ancient reservoir that had served the development needs of the Oddichuddan region. The legend of the Than Thonriya Lingam as I heard it, was that a cultivator, while ploughing his fields stumbled on something hard which on excavation was found to be a Lingam buried in the ground.

The quest for the ancient reservoir was very successful. The remnants of the stupendous earthen embankments of the ancient Muthu Rayan Kaddu Kulam were discerned in the jungle; we also found the remnants of a place of worship on the hilltop and the broken adukku Kallu anicut. These were reputed to have been erected originally during Kulakoddan's Vanni regime but evidently have been subsequently restored and later abandoned. The tank bund had a unique feature in that it had two large breaches obviously the work of human element and not due to natural calamity alone. Immediate steps were taken to restore the tank to serve as a major development project.

To continue the story of the Lingam: How did it happen to be there? The Linga Moorthy had been found by the cultivator whilst ploughing. Interesting stories have been told as to how the site became a place of holy worship. As folk lore would have it, it would appear that once upon a time four great religious asceties of profound veneration, came from India and lived in ashramams at the following places in Lanka: Thandavirayar at Pavaddi, Muthu Lingar at Kadirkamam, Tirukoner at Samalan Kulam and Kumarasuriar at Oddichuddan.

This may have happened separately at different times during the Vanni regime. Whatever that may have been, these places became hallowed and Siva Lingams installed there on the demise of the savants. Such a story can well account for finding a Siva Lingam in the gound without any other remnants or debris of a temple structure, at the site.

How the location got its name Oddichuddan (meaning where Kurakkan stumps were burnt) is an interesting story. Once a pioneer colonist from Iddai Kadu, in the Jaffna Peninsula, named Veerapathirar cleared jungle and settled down here. Noticing that Kurakkan stumps around a perticular konral tree does not burn, he and others improvised a Vinayaka shrine there and it was in close proximity to this that Linga Murthy did reveal himself to the cultivator as already mentioned.

He thus earns the name of Veka Vana Iswaran (Lord from the jungle that does not burn) and His consort is Puloka Nayaki.

Navaratnam says in his 'Short History of Hinduism' 'The Vanniya chieftain of that principality soon founded a temple to Than Thontry Iswarar at the site where the 'LINGAM' was first discovered. Later on, some enterprising Government Officers who served in the district and other well-wishers rebuilt this venerable house of God'.

So today we have an old temple at Oddichuddan where the venerable Linga Moorthy in the sanctum is found presiding from ground level. I paid homage to the Lord on several occasions during the years 1948-1950.

The far flung temple building and the large spacious Therppai Kulam are an attraction but they need repairs and maintenance to retain them in good condition.

The annual festival commences on new moon day in the month of Ani and lasts fifteen days. The Veddai (going-a-hunting) thiruvila on the thirteenth day is a unique festive occasion for all young and old. In performing their vows, band of over five hundred persons, decked in Veddah array display their prowess, finishing up with a dip in the beautiful Therppai Kulam. The car festival and theertham on the full moon day attract large crowds from the neighbouring villages.

With the development works of the Muthu Iyan Kaddu Kulam project, fresh life has come to the village. Oddichuddan is no longer a neglected out-post of the Vanni.

Reference:

Song compositions have been prepared about this temple, by Kuhathaser S. Sabaretna Mudaliyar 1883, and Pandithar A. S. Nagalingam.

30. THIRUKETHEESWARAM TEMPLE, MANNAR

Thiruketheeswaram near Mannar is the scene where Hindus congregate in large numbers on Sivarathiri night; they gather in thousands and tens of thousands to worship the Lord of Thiruketheeswaram.

The site became hallowed in mythology, for here Kethu sought refuge to perform penance, beseeching the Supreme Iswara, thus giving the place its name of Thiru-Keethu-Iswaram. Tradition has it that a temple was built at Thiruketheeswaram by Mayan, father-in-law of Ravana the Emperor of Sri Lankapura to install a Siva Lingam, the object of veneration of the Emperor's Queen.

Historically the settlement is recorded to have been an important sea-port where International Trade flourished. Here the Chinese from the East, with their jars of oils met the Babylonians and the Egyptians from the West, with their glass and beads for bartering their goods; it would have been a veritable supermarket - a Maha Santhai or Mantai for short. The place also won for itself the name of Mahatitta or the great landing place, as referred to in the Mahawamsa.

Five tiered Gopuram—Thiruketheeswaram

With a water-course flowing by, the luxurious fertility of the place must have been alluring as could be seen in the descriptions in the Thevarams (psalms) sung about the place and the temple, by Saints Thirugnanasampanthar and Suntharar.

The area still retains the name of Matoddam or Maha-Thoddam or the settlement established by Maha Thuvadda the Visvakarma King, at the behest of the Lord.

During the time of the great Chola King Rajaraja I, Thiruketheeswaram was named Rajaraja-Iswaram and a magnificent temple was standing majestically with several Gopurams and Prakarams amidst a big city and settlement. Remnants and ruins of brickwork found today, remind us of the glorious days of the past.

With the destruction of the temple in 1589, the area reverted to jungle until Arumuga Navalar's clarion call in 1872. This urged S. T. M. Pasupathy Chettiyar to undertake excavations at the site and unearth the celebrated Maha Lingam and Nandi in June 1894. Thereupon religious worship became restored at this sacred Hindu sthalam, with a humble shrine on 28th June, 1903. A temple of modest proportions was however soon erected in 1910, which the Nagarathar, a Chetty community, devotedly cherished and maintained for seveal years.

Recent revival commenced with V. K. Sellapah Swamy tracing the ancient Palavi water course and the restoration of Palavi theertham in 1949. A Temple Restoration Society was then formed, which very soon devoted itself to making all necessary arrangements for the building of a proper traditional Sivan Kovil, with two praharas, for Gowri Ambal sametha Katheeswaranathar. This stupendous task was ably and devotedly spearheaded by Sir Kandiah Vaithianathan. Foundations for the structures were laid in 1953 and construction work proceeded thereafter culminating with the performance of the Maha Kumba Abishekam ceremonies on 4th July 1976.

Thiruketheeswaram-Temple Towers

There is now a majestic Siva Devasthanam at this revered ancient sthalam, complete with all the prahara murthi temples and with the Siva Linga Murthi and Gowri Ambal presiding in the main moolasthanam. Thousands of devotees gather there for the annual Sivarathiri festival from all over the Island. They all perform the much coveted 'Theertha Kavadi Maha Linga Abishekam' themselves and witness the resplendent Lingotpavar puja at midnight.

The Maha Lingam at Thiruketheeswaram Temple, Mannar
Devotee awaits tharisanam during puja.

Comprehensive information on the subject is found in the Author's book, titled, 'The Lord of Thiruketheeswaram', 1980.

Other published literature:

'Thiruketheeswaram Papers'—Sir Kandiah Vaithianathan
'Thiruketheeswaram' by A. Kandiah, in Tamil
'Thiruketheeswara Puranam', in Tamil

31. KONESWARAM SIVAN TEMPLE, TRINCOMALEE

It was in the year 1950, on the 27th of July, when to the workmen who were digging a well for tenements in the North Coast Road in the heart of Trincomalee town, were revealed the Somaskandar, Ambal and Sandirasekera Moorthies of excellent bronze of the celebrated Koneswaram Temple.

Koneswaram is an ancient Hindu sthalam of antiquity. The story of ancient Lankapuram abounds with legends, myths and traditions like that of any other land. Similarly tradition persists strongly associating ancient Koneswaram with Emperor Ravana and his worship of the sacred Siva Lingam; for at Koneswaram (Kon-Iswaram, Kon— King or Supreme one) was built a temple for Iswaran or God Parameswaran. Dr. Paul E. Pieris, the eminent scholar, records in R. A. S. Journal that even during the pre-historic days there were five Iswaran Temples in Lanka dedicated to Lord Parameswara of which one was at Koneswaram. Here congregated pilgrims, not only from Lanka but from India as well, for the Darshan of the Lord. But the temple was probabley demolished along with other temples, in the third century.

Thither came Chola Kankan, grand son of Chola King Manu Neethi Kankan. He had come for the observance of certain vows undertaken by his parents who became blessed with a son and heir after their pilgrimage to this celebrated sthalam. On seeing the temple of his dreams in ruins he dedicated himself to **his life mission**, viz: the restoration of the temple at Koneswaram and building a tank for watering the temple paddy lands - thus becoming immortalised with the name-title of Kulakoddan - the builder of tank and temple. Persons well versed in agricultural pursuits developed the area. Pallava culture and civilisation made the area flourish, and the temple also became an outstanding place of worship. The name and fame of Koneswara Nathar inspired Thiru Gnana Sampanthar, one of the Samayachchariar Hindu Saints, who lived in the seventh century, to offer a garland of Thevaram out-pourings in a pathikam of verses, thus elevating the place to a 'padal petta Sthalam 'status, earning the name of Dakshana Kailayam or Kailash of the South.

The Cholas and Pandyas paid homage to the Lord of Koneswaram. Sunderapandyan (1251-1280), who built several temples, had an architectural edifice 'with a thousand pillars' erected for Koneswarar, the description of which is gleaned from Portuguese documents.

Aruna Kiri Nathar visited the place in the 15th century and offered a pathiham garland of Thirupuhal verses.

Several Moorthies of superb workmanship must have adorned such a temple, judging from the icons discovered by the workmen in 1950.

Detailed description of these and others found later are given in a talk delivered by Dr. W. Balendra, before the Royal Asiatic Society in 1952.

Nothing of the old temple, however, remains today (except for a single pillar stone seen in the picture) as the temple and all its structures were blasted into the sea by the

Portuguese, under the direction of Constantine de Saa, on the Hindu New Year day, in the year 1624.

The site remained an empty rock for several years and devotees worshipped and made their offerings facing the ocean. The findings of 1950, however, caused a wave of resurgence and steps were taken to erect a new Sivan Kovil Temple at the site, which was completed and Kumba-Abishekam ceremonies performed on the 3rd of April, 1963. It is a grand structure as the photo taken by me shortly after 1963, shows.

Koneswaram rebuilt, 1963   The Dakshana Kailayam of the ancients

The ancient Thiru-Murthy Vigrakams which were unearthed in 1950, mentioned earlier, have been installed prominently in the new temple.

The Thirukona Nayakar-Somaskanda Murthy is an excellent Chola bronze icon over a foot and a half by a foot in size and weighs over half a hundred-weight. The Mathumai Ambal Devi is exquisite and is cast to match the Somaskanda Vigraham. The Vinayaka icon which was also recovered is unusually large.

The Sandirasekara Murthy, probably of an earlier period, and Parvathi Ambal in Thiruvanka pose, were the other bronzes recovered.

Regular pujas and festivals are held in the temple today.

Among the Publicatons on Koneswaram are:

'Trincomalee Bronzes', R. A. S. Journal 1952, Dr. W. Balendra
'Thirukonesar Alaya Kumba-Abisheka Malar', 1963 (Tamil)
'Thirukoneswara' (Tamil), Pulavar V. Somaskandar and A. Sriskandarajah, 1963
'Koneswaram' (Tamil), S. Gunasingam, Peradeniya, 1973

32. AGASTIYAR STHAPANAM, KANKUVELI, KILIVEDDI
(OLD SIVAN KOVIL AT THIRU KARASAI)

In the outskirts of Kankuveli, a village in Kottiyaram, Trincomalee District, is a venerated site, marked 'Koviltirumadu Ruins' on the maps, associated with the legendary visit of Agastiyar to the Southern regions—as mentioned in 'The Dakshana Kailasa Puranam' of old.

The Kovil Thiru Madu, as its name implies is a villu or low ground, replenished by water from the Mahaweli Ganga which flows by whenever the Ganga is in flood. Here it is said, was founded the hallowed legendary city of Karasai, of the Thiru Karasai Puranam.

The source of the legend is the 'Thiru Karasai Puranam' of 170 verses, an old puranam, which V. Akilesapillai had first published in 1893; it has since been republished in 1952 by A. Alahakoon; it extols the blessedness of the sacred Karasiumpathy Siva Lingam installed at Agastiyar Sthapanam by the banks of the Mahaweli Ganga.

The story of the legend narrates how all the Gods and Goddesses of the Hindu pantheon, the Devas, devotees, and others had assembled at Kailash to witness the divine wedding of Sivahamy Ambal to Lord Siva. The large assembly congregating there caused a precarious position and Lord Siva asked sage Agastiyar to leave and go down South, for balancing the load. The dimunitive Munivar was promised that he would neverthless be blessed with the vision of the divine nuptials, from there. The sage visiting several known places of Hindu pilgrimage, was, wending his way, south, towards Thiru Konesam, the Dakshana Kailasam of the day ; but realising that even there, the Divine wedding ceremonies would be celebrated, stops south of it, along the banks of the Mahaweli Ganga, thereby making that place and the Ganga, sacred. At this site was founded the Karasai city with the full complement of temples for the worship of Lord Siva; for, was this not the place from where the sage saw the Divine Nuptials of Kailash? The site ever since gains the name of Agasthiyar Sthapanam, with the Lord presiding at the Temple as Tiru Karasium Pathy Shiva Linga Moorthy.

It becomes a venerated place and tradition says here did Sri Lakshmi Devi come to perform thapas for the safe return of Her divine Consort Vishnu, when he undertook the difficult mission of up rooting the world's evils from the bottom of the sea, taking a marine form.

Ages and ages later, King Singaputhan, resting here on the banks of the Ganga, after traversing several miles having lost everything in the battlefield, finds solace. On divine directions he marries Thirumankai the daughter of the local king and recovers his possessons and his kingdom. He rebuilds the temple for the Lord at Tiru Karasai, the worship of whom had helped to recover his kingly position. South of the Agastiyar Sthapanam temple are found the well preserved ruins of a stone masonry temple structure, known as 'Thiru Mankalai Alaiyam', said to have been founded by Thirumankai, Queen of King Singaputhan.

The meandering Ganga has since shifted its course and the river is found away from the temple; today at the site is found an ancient Siva Lingam, with a round avudaiyar; its central rudra paham shaft is somewhat damaged and therefore covered with a piece of cloth. The Nanthi appears intact. An attractive, but damaged Subramaniya Moorthi is also found. A large stone inscription is also found standing upright at the site. Broken walls, steps and other pieces of masonary are found scattered in the locality.

An interesting episode, marrated locally is the story of the foolish hunter who attempted to sharpen his blunt knife on the crest of the abandoned Siva Lingam, mistaking it for an ordinary stone. Lo! He went blind immediately. Later, in attonement for his folly, he became a keen devotee of the Lord, and re-instituted worship there.

Once a year, on new moon day of the month of Adi (July-August) the folks from the nearby village of Kankuveli celebrate a theertham festival at this place, bringing the moorthi from Kankuveli Sivan Temple. The day is spent bathing in the Ganga, having puja ceremonies and reading the Tiru Karasai Puranam, after which they return home. The link with the Agastiyar legend is thus preserved.

Reference:

'Thiru Karasai Puranam' in Tamil, 1893
'Thiru Konesala Vaipavam' in Tamil, by V. Ahilesapillai, 1889

33. MUNESWARAM TEMPLE, CHILAW

One of the celebrated five very ancient temples for worship of Lord Iswara is Muneswaram temple; it is situated about a mile east of Chilaw. In the era of hoary antiquity this Munna Natha Iswaram with the chief deity Munna Natha Lingam, so Dakshana Kailasa Puranam (Ch 16) says, was established by Brahma for worship by Himself, Vishnu Mahendran, munivars, sages and seers.

Sri Rama Bhagavan is said to have found solace here, on his return journey home after the Ramayana episode with a heavily weighted conscience thinking of the many deaths in the battles. He experienced relief from the 'Brama Sakthy' that had worried him; so he stopped here and performed pujas and other ceremonies.

Tradition has it that Queen Alli Arasani, who reigned during the ancient days, was emphatic on making three separate heaps of the proceeds of pearl fishery, one for Sri Meenakshi of Mathurai Temple, another for Sri Vadivambikai of Muneswaram Temple, and the third for herself. It was also one of the temples renovated by Prince Vijaya after being crowned king of Lanka, for the benefit of his subjects. It is also claimed to have been improved and maintained by Kulakoddan and by the Cholas during their occupation of the Island.

The temple flourished due to the munificence of King Parakrama Bahu VI (1412-1467) who gifted several villages and paddy lands. The reputed wealth of the temple attracted the greed of the Portuguese invaders who destroyed and razed it to the ground in the year 1578.

However, Vadivambikai Ambal sametha Munna Nathar could not remain dormant for long. About 200 years later, the temple was restored for worship by King Kirti Raja Singhe, in 1753. Later it was renovated in 1875, by efforts made by Brahma Sri Cumaraswamy Kurukkal; it was improved in 1919 and further in 1963 with support offered by Hindus, all over Ceylon. It was renovated recently and a Gopuram was also provided.

The annual festival at this temple lasts for twenty-seven days terminating with the water-cutting ceremony, on the full-moon day in the month of avany (August-September), in Mayavan Aru (Dedura Oya).

A special feature at Muneswaram is the nine-day Navarathiri festival which occurs in October. Elaborate ceremonies are observed during these nine days, more profound and impressive, than at any other temple in Sri Lanka. Among the items included in these observances are the daily Chanka abishekam with 108 chanks, khumba puja, special yaga, chanting of vedas and other ceremonies that last a full day. On Vijaya Thasamy day, Vadivambikai Ambal is taken in procession, for the Manampu festival.

Published Literature

There have been several publicatons on the subject, most of them in Tamil, some of which are:

'Sri Muneswara Manmiam', Brama Sri M. Somaskanda Kurukal, 1949
'Sri Muneswara Varalaru', P. Siva Rama Krishna Sharma 1968
Three celebrated poets have composed 'The Unjal Paddu' songs.
Several others have written in praise of Vadivambikai Ambal.

34. RAMA LINGA ISWARAN TEMPLE, MAHA MANAWERIYAWA, CHILAW

About six miles to the north of Chilaw on the road to Puttalam, there stands an old Sivan Temple, near the Manaweriyawa Estate, a, humble temple dedicated to the worship of Sri Rama Lingam.

The story of the Ramayana and the advent of Sri Rama Bhagavan to this Island is firmly rooted in the traditions of Sri Lanka.

With holy reverence, several places yet retain their association with Sri Ramar's presence. Muneswaram near Chilaw and Villundi in Jaffna are two such places.

Refernce is made in the Dakshana Kailasa Puranam (Ch. 17), how on Lord Parameswara's directons, Sri Rama Bhagawan instituted a Siva Sthalam at Manavery by the banks of the Ganga (Deduru Oya) and installed a Rama Lingam for worship by devotees, seeking solace.

Rama Linga Iswaran Temple Manaweriyawa

In the small sanctum of the temple is the Iswara Lingam, which has sunk low in the absence of a proper Avudayar. The Linga Moorthy resembles the Lingams of the Chola era found in Lanka. The temple structure, seen today, was built about a hundred years ago and has the frontal appearance of North Indian shrines. The prahara moorthies and the Vaganams found in the Mandapams all require attention. Pujas are performed daily in the evenings, and in the mornings as well on Fridays. There are no lands endowed to the temple and the management has only the support of about ten Hindu families resident in the vicinity for maintaining it. The Trustee M. Arunasalam is obviously finding it hard. A therppaikulam has also been made in the vicinity.

Annually a four day festival is held, coinciding with Thai Poosam day in January. The deity is taken in procession to the neighbouring villages in turn.

35. PONNAMBALAVANESWARAR TEMPLE, COLOMBO
(RAMANATHAN SIVAN KOVIL)

During my young days, when I was studying at St. Thomas' College, I was a regular devotee of this temple from 1920 onwards. Residing in the neghbourhood, I used to spend long hours watching the South Indian craftsmen chisel and carve out fine elaborate shapes and figures, in granite, that form the Sivan temple erected by Sir P. Ramanathan at Korteboam Street, Kochchikade. Work on the erection of a proper Sivan Kovil, in carved granite stone masonry, conforming in every detail to modern Madurai style of Dravidian architecture was commenced in 1907.

Ponnambalavan Eswarar Temple, Colombo
(Ramanathan Sivan Kovil)
Interior is in Sculptural Stonework of traditional architecture

His father, Gate Mudaliyar Arunasalam Ponnambalam, a celebrated person of his time, founded a temple at the site, originally, in the year 1856, at the behest of several residents of the area. It was managed by his eldest son Pon. Cumaraswamy after which Sir P. Ramanathan took on the management and in 1907 decided to re-build the small Sivan Kovil into a magnificent gem of architecture. Work was necessarily slow as it entailed heavy expenditure and the movement of boat loads of granite stones, suitable for architectural work. The temple as completed in 1912 has two praharas, containing the garba graham for the presiding Maha Lingam, Ambal shrine and the stipulated prahara moorthy shrines. The pillars and sculptures are superb. The Raja gopuram is a recent addition during the trusteeship of Sir A. Mahadeva.

It has been described by Kalai Pulavar K. Navaratnam, in his book on 'Development of Art in Ceylon', 1955, as an, 'Architectural edifice worthy of mention, built during the British period .... The temple is built of stone ... The pillars and sculptures are of the type found in modern temples of South India. The temple may be considered the 'Architectural gem of South Indian Art in Ceylon today. Visitors to the country pay a visit to this temple'.

A well organised management attends to the careful performance of all pujas and other rites to be done at a Sivan temple. In addition to the two annual festivals, other special occasions are observed carefully. The Maha Sivarathiri, occuring in February-March is a very special occasion, when all Colombo congregates there all night to witness the abishekams and the pujas at the four watches of the night.

36. SIVAN TEMPLES (IN RUINS) AT POLONNARUWA

The ruins of eight Hindu Temples or rather groups of Hindu Temples have been unearthed at Polonnaruwa. They belong to the medieval period, of the Chola era and have been excavated during the years 1901 onwards.

These temples, large and small, have been erected in conformity with traditional requirements of temple construction. Of these, three of them were of granite stone masonry and the others of brickwork. The stone temples had their superstructure or vimanam in brickwork. All of them had stone pillars.

At most of the Sivan Temples, the moolasthana Siva Lingam can be seen, though damaged and in parts. Majority of them have a square or rectangular avudaiyar but three of them are circular in shape.

In the precincts, if not, in the immediate vicinity of each temple, there is also a Vishnu Kovil.

In the praharam of all these temples, a separate shrine (in brickwork) for Vinayakar is also found - invariably the figure of Vinayakar is also to be seen at the site. Ruins of separate shrines of Subramaniyar and Bhairava Moorthies are found only at some of the temples.

A description of some of these temples is given here. For fuller information, readers may refer to the Reports of the Archaeological Commissioner, published as Government Sessional Papers from 1901 onwards from which most of what appears below have been collected.

Siva Devale No. 1

This veritable gem of architecture and superb sculpture is found close to Polonnaruwa town, off the Habarana Road.

The nine foot, almost square, garbagraham with a small antralam and the 60 ft. by 40 ft. Maha Mandapam were all of granite stones dressed and moulded to a high order of workmanship, ornate with niches, pilasters and other decorative works of sculpture.

In the niches of the walls are seen figures (though damaged) of Ambal of marvellous sculpture; the pleat formation and the pedestal are noteworthy. A four foot high statue of Sivahamy Ambal is now preserved at the Polonnaruwa Museum.

A point of interest, in passing, is the incomplete or bare finish of ornate work on the bases and capitals of the pilasters in the northern wing in contrast with those of the southern wing.

The prahara murthikal shrines of Vinayakar and Subramaniyar and Bhairavar had been in brickwork, unlike the main temple structure.

Siva Devale No 1, Polonnaruwa, a veritable gem of medieval architecture

The avudaiyar of the Siva Lingam assembled and placed in the sanctum is about 30 inches square; the girth of the Lingam axle is about 20 inches.

Homage at Siva Devale No. 1, Polonnaruwa

A set of bronze icons found buried, and which are how housed in the Colombo Museum, are veritable masterpieces of Chola art, reaching a standard of perfection acknowledged as the highest in Ceylon or even in India. These include an Anandha

Nadarasar Vigrakam 36 inches in height, which is outstanding, a Somaskanda Moorthy pose, two Ambals, and the saints Appar Swamikal and Manicka Vasaga Swamikal. A comprehensive description and enlightenment on their symbolism was given by Sir P. Arunachalam in a talk to the Royal Asiatic Society - vide R. A. S. Journal No. 68, 1915-1916.

The better degree of preservation of the temple structure and the finer embellishments that enrich the architectural and sculptural finish of the temple structure all indicate a later period of origin of this temple.

Siva Devale No. 2

The temple of Vanavan Mahadevi Isvaramudaiyar, Lord of Jana Natha Mandalam

This beautiful Chola temple is the only structure of the Hindu temples at Polonnaruwa where occasional worship is performed. On the Ani Uthiram day in June large gathering assembles here for observances and worship organised by the Pulasthipura Maha Jana Sabai, Polonnaruwa. This festival has now been held for over fifteen years in arrangement with the Government Archaeological Department.

Siva Devale No 2, Polonnaruwa, a Chola temple identified by the inscriptions on the walls

The unique feature of this temple is the Tamil inscriptions found on the walls of the structure which identifies it beyond any doubt.

The garbagraham is about nine foot square and the antralam is slightly less. The walls which rise from the square base are decorated with pilasters with niches between them. There are Kudus at intervals. A three-tiered vimanam is found terminating with an octogonal sthoopi at the top. The whole structure is built of granite and limestone in lime mortar, as will be seen in the illustration.

Besides the main structure, there had been also two shrines, about 8ft. square at the south-west and the north-west corners, in brickwork.

The sacred Lingam installed in the Moolasthanam can be seen today at the site. The avudaiyar is square and the Rudra Pakam (axle) is eight inches in diameter and stands out more than one and a half feet high.

The Inscriptions

The shorter inscriptions on the western wall refer to the installation of Pallikondar and Sri Alagiya Mana Valar in the temple of the Vanavan Mahadevi Isvaramudaiyar and praises King Rajendra Cholan.

The twenty-three line long inscription found on the exterior of the southern wall, mentions the name of the temple and the name of the Chola King Adhi Rajendra Deva and the granting of money for maintaining a lamp and lamp stand at the temple of Vanavan Mahadevi Isvaramudaiyar, Lord of Jana Natha Mandalam.

These lead to fixing this temple to the period of reign of Rajendra Cholan about 1012-1044. A. C.

Siva Devale No. 5

This most interesting temple, situated on the Road to Anaivulanda has yielded the largest number and most exquisitely worked bronzes, of supreme workmanship and art.

The main structure and a similar but smaller structure of Vishnu are built adjoining each other. Entrance is gained by a porch which is equivalent to a Gopuram, portions of which have been excavated. The site is easily the largest Hindu Temple at Polonnaruwa. A rectangular wall encloses the temple premises. The main building is more elaborate than the other temples and has additional mandapams. The garbha-graha is about 9 ft. square, and there are two vestibules, an inner and an outer artha mandapams. These are fronted by two Maha Mandapams. There is in addition an exterior Vasantha Mandapam, and a large reception hall built transverse. The whole structure is in brickwork, with the pilasters mouled in lime mortar.

Of special interest is the upper portion of the Vimanam; the sthoopi or dome of the Vimanam built of brick work with good mortar, is found intact, fallen on the ground behind the shrine. It still shows the frieze that had been worked all around.

The traditional shrine for Vinayakar is found at the South-West corner; the separate shrine by the Artha Mandapam and facing south would obviously be the Ambal Kovil. Similarly placed structure further east would be that of the Nadaraja Moorthy.

The chief presiding deity of this celebrated temple is the Lingeswara Moorthy. A granite damaged statue of the Lingam unearthed at the spot is assembled there. The Brahma Peedam, 3 foot square, is there; the intermediate Vishnu Peedam with the octogonal socket is missing. The Rudra Paham consisting of the vertical shaft is superb in appearance.

This temple was excavated in 1908 and the Archaeological Commissioner's Annual Report for 1908, contains a detailed report. The list of statues and bronzes found in 1908 is by itself a most interesting document. The Report is published as Government Sessional Papers No. VI of 1913.

Sir Ponnambalam Arunachalam made an inspiring contribution to the Royal Asiatic Society, Ceylon, in 1915 on this subject, as already referred to earlier under Siva Devale No. 1. He describes and further aids the study of these. He identifies the bronzes and describes the symbols they represent. His contribution has placed the entire subject at a high level and has to be gratefully acknowledged today as a source of inspiration. The reader is referred to R. A. S. Journal, Vol. XXIV, No. 68 which contains his address. In his opinion 'The bronzes are characterised by the precision that comes of long tradition and practice .... and are a music to the eye'.

Further finds were made during the 1960 excavations, as reported by Dr. C. E. Godakumbara at a lecture before the R. A. S. - vide their Journal Vol. VIII, Part 2 (New Series) of 1961. He said that behnid the Devale, close to the fallen Vimanam and sthoopi was found a 3 feet deep pit about 5 feet by 3 feet in which were found several bronzes, all well arranged in order. It is reported that among the finds in the pit, 'an earthen censor with charcoal in it bore silent testimoney to a final ritual accompanied with the burning of incense'. The neighbourhood yielded other finds; among the statues found were: Nadaraja nearly 6 ft. high, Somaskanda Murthy, Sivakamy Ambal, Karaikkal Ammaiyar, Vinayakar and Maha Vishnu.

Other Devales

The other Siva Devales are smaller temples. Siva Devale No. 3 has stonework with sharp ornamentation and may be of a later period. S. D. No. 6, situated about one mile away may be the earliest as much weathering is evident.

My reverence to these commenced in the year 1946, when I used to live at Minneriya.

Reference:

Government Sessional Papers and R. A. S. Journals as indicated in the text.

37. THAN THONRIYA ISWARAN TEMPLE, KOKKADICHOLAI, BATTICALOA

An ancient Sivan temple in Batticaloa is the Than Thonriya Iswaran temple at Kokkadicholai, about ten miles south of Batticaloa. It is reached by travelling seven miles to Manmunai, crossing by ferry and proceeding about two miles.

The Linga Moorthy, which is the presiding deity of the temple, is fondly referred to by the local community as Than Thonriya Appa, in view of its legendary origin. During the reign of Kuna Singam in Batticaloa, there was Ulaga Nachchi Ammaiyar, a Kalinga Princess, who was chief of this region. One day, a person called Thidahan, who was working in the jungle, saw a tree which was dripping drop by drop. He ran and conveyed this unsual phenomenon to the Princess and Ulaga Nachchi Ammaiyar proceeded to the site and on examination found a Siva Lingam at the foot of the tree. As it defied their attempts at removal, the Princess had a shrine erected around that Kokku Neddi tree.

Tradition associates the building of a temple here to the period of Kalinga Magha (1215-1255), who was a staunch Saivaite King. The sthoopi remains today to remind us of the past. S. Pathmanathan in his 'The Kingdom of Jaffna' (p. 119) observes that 'the architectural style of the Vimanam of this temple, which was dominated by its massive sthupi and was of brick construction and the Pandya style of architecture seems to suggest that the temple had been constructed on an elaborate scale during the thirteenth century'. In the notes, he adds further, that 'The other parts of the original structures have vanished in course of time. The mandapam and the surrounding subsidiary shrines are recent constructions'.

In the sixteenth century the temple had been threatened with destruction by the foreign invaders, like so many other Hindu temples. But the story of a striking incident that occurred then is cherished by everyone ever since. The invaders had demanded from the temple Poshakar the purpose or use of the Nandi Bull seen at the entrance and if it can eat grass or drink water. When they were told it can, they challenged them and to their utter dismay, the inanimate Nandi Devar munched the grass that was offered and took in the theertham. Such was faith and its glories that it works miracles even to this day.

Today the temple is well maintained and Than Thonri Appa enjoys regular customary pujas and other ceremonies. The annual fifteen day festival terminates with full moon day in the month of August. Two majestic rathams are taken out for procession on the car-festival day and customary payments in kind are made at the end. On the next day is the ceremonial theertham, and boar-hunting festival, to amuse the congeregation present.

Daily during the festival season can be seen many amateur old-world dramatic performances, for which the locality is renowned.

38. NAGULESWARAM, KEERIMALAI, JAFFNA

An ancient place of Hindu worship along the northern sea coast was Nakules-waram.

Naguleswaram, at Keerimalai near Kankesanturai, has been declared by the eminent scholar and historian Dr. Paul E. Pieris (ref 1) as being one of the 'five recognised iswarams of Siva, that were in Lanka, long before the arrival of Vijaya (543 B.C.) and which claimed and received adoration of all India'. How this sthalam, became to be known as Naguleswaram is attributed to it having been the residence of a Munivar whose abode had been a local cave inside which he lived his life of penance, states M. D. Raghavan (ref 2).' 'It is said that he got so shrunk by age and austerities that he was likened to a mongoose' - Nakula, in Sanskrit and Keeri, in Tamil. Hence the name Naguleswaram for the sthalam and Keerimalai for the rock with the cave in it.

Entrance to a cave in the rock

The Sthalam had been known even to tradition as a sacred theertham, bathing in which aids the remission of sins that accumulate due to Karma. For this same purpose, the Maha Bharatam mentions that celebrated personages Musukun-than, Nalla Maha Raja, Arujuna and several others made their pilgrimages to the sacred sthalam and having bathed in the spring waters that pour out from the caves, made their obeisance before Naguleswari Ambal and Naguleswara Nathar, requesting boons.

The Keerimalai theertha kerney has been well built and renovated recently, with several additions and improvements and is very well patronised. Hindus from all over gather here, on the new moon day in July, for dipping in the sacred waters and pay obeisance to the departed souls. The Magam day in February is also another important festival day.

Another legend frequently associated with the place is the Maha Bharata story of Jamathakiri, who incurred the displeasure of sage Pituku Munivar by not placating him, after having invited him for the observance of ancestral ceremonies. For this, she had to suffer a curse which changed her facial appearance to that of a 'Keeri'; this disappeared when she performed abolutions in the sacred fresh spring waters of Naguleswaram, when the curse was lifted. The rocky place thereby became known as Nagula Kiri rock or simply Kiri-Malai and today Keerimalai.

The celebrated ancient Keerimalai can be seen by walking about half a mile along the beach.

Whatever, that may have been, we know for certain that the spring water flow at Keerimalai is of great value and bathing in its waters imparts therapeutic medicinal benefit to the human body. From its source in the rocks of Tellipallai-Maviddapuram (30 feet elevation) area, the spring waters flowing through the crevices and fissures of the carbonated rocks, encountering sea water as it emerges at Keerimalai, acquire chemical values and minute electrolytic charges, which tonic the functioning of the human system.

The name and fame of the sthalam spread far and wide. In the 15th century, we read in history, that Bhuvenaka Bahu, the celebrated King who built Nallur Kandaswamy Temple, visited this theertham, and having paid obeisance to the Lord of Naguleswaram, took charge of the place, for maintenance by the State.

However, subsequently the temple suffered the same fate of demolition as that of all Hindu temples, in the hands of foreigners of the seventeenth century.

Today one can see the celebrated spring and the rock on which the old temple stood, by proceeding about half a mile along the beach towards Kankesanturai, from Keerimalai.

The renaissance of Hinduism by Arumuga Navalar, in the latter part of the nineteenth century, saw the rebuilding of several temples that were demolished earlier.

The present Sivan Temple for the Lord of Naguleswaranathar and Naguleswari Ambal was built in 1859. It is a beautiful temple carefully administered by its management. Impressive moorthies adorn the decorated sanctum. Several devotees attend the fifteen day annual festival ending with Sivarathiri in February-March for darshan of the Lord and Ambal. Improvement works are being carried out gradually, with incoming finances.

Recently the interior walls have been painted depicting legendary Hindu Puranic episodes. An eye-catching one is the painting depicting the mythological churning of the milky ocean by the Devas in search of 'Amirtham', the elixir of perpetual life. A grand Rajagopuram is a recent undertaking.

Regular pujas are held daily and all the Hindu festivals observed carefully. The Annual Mahotsava Festival in the month of February-March terminates with the observance of the Sivarathri Festival and the 'Theertham' ceremony the following morning.

Keerimalai is today a place of worship and holy reverence; thousands of devotees flock here to have their expiatory baths.

Reference:

1.   Pieris, Paul E., 'Nagadipa and Budhist Remains in Jaffna', J. R. A. S. (CB) Vol. XXVIII No. 12, p. 68 & Vol. XXV No. 70 pp 17-18

2.   Raghava, M. D., 'Tamil Culture in Ceylon', 1966, p. 239

39. URUTHIRAPURI ISWARAN TEMPLE, KILINOCHCHI

Uruthirapuram and Uruthiraperumkulam (or Uttaraperumkulam) have been landmarks in the Uttaradasa ancient Northern territory of the Island. History narrates the story how Nagadeepa in Northern Lanka, was once flourishing with Kathiramali its chief city, enjoying trade and commerce with the ancient Greeks and Romans.

Attracted by the well - being of the region, several settlers migrated here from across Palk Strait. The Kalingas were a community who settled down in the northern parts of the Island's mainland. The region was outside the region of the Anuradhapura Kings and earned the name of Uttara Desa.

The region flourished and in its glorious days had its settlements, temples and tanks. Today we are reminded of this one time 'Glory' with names that linger such as Uttira-perumkulam and Uttirapuri Iswaran Kovil. The Kalingas grew strong and even contested the Anuradhapura Kings and the Naga Kingdom of the North. That would have been during the eras of about the sixth to the eighth centuries. They were friendly with the Chola power in Ceylon. Eventually they were overcome by the Pandyans who invaded Nagadeepa and Anuradhapura as well.

The ancient Siva Linga Murthi, of several centuries past, unearthed on the 2nd of September 1882 and installed in August 1958, now presides majestically at this Sivan Temple. The square Avudaiyar is indicative of Chola origin.

This celebrated place of old came to notice, with the discovery of a Siva Lingam and some ruins of a Sivan temple in the Kilinochchi jungles, off Kunchu Paranthan, on the 2nd of September 1882. On the advice of Sir William Twynam, the then Government Agent, the Lingam was removed, for safekeeping to the Amman Kovil nearby.

Later, with the development of the area as Uruthiraperumkulam Colonisation Scheme, the colonists partially built a Sivan Kovil and installed the ancient Siva Lingam, with the short Rudra Paham and ornamental rectangular avudaiyar, in the sanctum, in the year 1958.

The devotees are able, once again, to worship and make obeisance to Uruthirapurieswaran, as in the early days of Ceylon history.

Efforts are now being made to build up the temple as a complete agamic Sivan Kovil.

40. KONAINAYAKAR TEMPLE, TAMPALAKAMAM

The story of the famous Koneswaram temple at Thirukonamalai has been narrated earlier. It is said that when that majestic edifice was threatened with demolition by the foreign invaders, the priests and the pandaram workers of the temple, escaped taking with them the precious deities Konainayakar and Madumai Ambal, and some valuable articles. These were installed at a place called Kalani malai, says the 'Thiru Konesala Vaipavam' (ref 1). That was in the year 1624.

Konainayakar Temple Gopuram Tampalakamam

Some years later King Rajasinha II (1635-1687) erected a proper temple at Tampalakamam for housing the deities taken from Koneswaram, and called the new shrine the Konainayakar Temple, Tampalakamam. Thus commenced another place of Hindu worship.

The temple is well endowed and has been well managed.

Reference:

1. 'Thiru Konesala Vaipavam', V. Akilesapillai 1889, p. 75

2. Navaratnam C. S. 'A Short History of Hinduism' 1962, p. 59

41. KAILASA NATHAR SIVAN TEMPLE, CAPTAIN'S GARDEN, COLOMBO

During the Dutch regime in Ceylon, a Chetty community from 'Thiruvilanga Nadu' in S. India, had settled down in Captain's Garden area in Colombo, engaged in mercantile activity.

It is said that a devoted worshipper at the Bala Selvavinayakar murthi temple at Captain's Garden Colombo, who was bereft of any offspring, made a vow; his vow was that he would erect a proper Sivan temple to house the Siva Linga murthi which was venerated under a tree in the garden. In course of time he was blessed with a son. The devotee, in fulfilment of his vow, erected the Kailasa Nathar Sivan Kovil and also named his son Kailasanathan.

The Chettiyar managing Trustee Board made several improvements and additions to the temple in 1933, making it a comprehensive agamic Sivan temple; Nanthies were provided at the Siva, Nadaraja and Ambal shrines; flagstaff was added and also five ther chariots for the five murthies, Pillaiyar, Sivan, Ambal, Subramaniyar and Chandikeswarar.

Besides the central mulasthana murthies, in the praharam there are prahara murthi temples for Vinayakar, Nadarajar, Subramaniyar, Maha Vishnu, Chandikeswarar, Saniyeswarar and the Navagraha deities. Within the temple are the Sandirasekera and Rajarajeswari murthi Vigrahams.

A notable feature here are the Kasi Viswanatha and the Kasi Visaladchi shrines, reminding the devotee of the holy institutions in Hinduism's most revered Kasi or Benarees.

There are also shrines for Brahma, Durga and Kali Amman in the northern pirahara.

Associated with the temple are madams for pilgrims and a school for children. The madam is a haven of rest for pilgrims enroute to Kathirkamam.

The temple and its temporalities are well managed. Regular pujas are held daily and all the festivals of a Sivan Temple are celebrated. Together with the adjoining Pillaiyar temple, the locality is visited by a constant stream of devotees.

42. ARUNACHALESVARAN SIVAN TEMPLE, MUTUWAL, COLOMBO

At Mutuwal or Mukathuwaram, where the river Kelani Ganga has its outflow into the ocean, in Colombo, is a venerable 'theerthakarai' Sivan Kovil. This Siva sthalam is a noble effort, for the well being of the Saiva community, built by Sir P. Arunachalam. This eminent personage of Hindu culture, learning and political leadership, was a younger brother of the notable personality Sir P. Ramanathan. Sir P. Arunachalam's book, titled 'Studies and Translations, Philosophical and Religious,' is a veritable gem of Hindu religion and culture, unlocking the treasures of the Hindu scriptures to the world. It also contains English translations of the scriptures and interpretations of the Saiva bronze vigraka statues.

The temple is spaciously laid out. The moolasthana Siva Lingam was brought from Kasi, Benarees and is installed here presiding as Arunachaleswara murthi. The divine consort is Parvatha Varthani Ambal. On either side of the sanctum are the entrance Vinayaka and Subramaniya shrines. The imposing Nadaraja murthi is housed in a separate shrine with an entrance facing the ocean. Another separate shrine is Kali Kovil, housing Kali Amman and Durga Devi Vigrahams. There are also the usual prahara murthies.

In keeping with the founder's high knowledge of Hindu agamic traditions, the pujas and festivals in the temple are observed meticulously and the descendants of the Arunchalam family successfully manage the temple's affairs. Religious classes enhance the Saiva culture of the children. An Interesting episode is the founder's association with a religious mendicant swamy named Anai kuddi swamikal. The swamy's high religious attainment had impressed Sir P. Arunachalam and there had been constant association. On the demise of the Swamiji, a Samadhi was erected here at this sacred theertha karai, a bathing ghat, where the waters meet.

43. RATNAPURI SABESAR SIVAN TEMPLE, RATNAPURA

A new Sivan Kovil has been built at Ratnapura on the advice of Guru Yoka Swamikal and Swamy Sangara Suppaiyar. Work was commenced on a plot of land donated by T. Velupillai in 1935. Many devotees, Hindus and others, including benefactor Thilliampalam worked hard and made valuable contributions to complete the structure in three years.

With the Kumba abishekam inauguration ceremony on the 8th of June 1938, Ratnapura, the city of Gems, was blessed with a Siva Devasthanam, patterned on the Visvanatha Temple at Benares. The heart of the temple is a four way mulasthana structure, at the centre of which the mula murthi Ratnapuri Sabesar presides with Thiripura Sunthari Ambal on His left. This sabai or hall arrangement is a unique feature of this temple and permits a closer approach to the deity, by the devotees. Santhirasekara, Maha Vishnu with his consorts, Brahma with Saraswathy and other deities are all found here.

In the praharam are found the traditional pari varaka murthi shrines of Vinayakar, Subramaniyar, Santhana Gopalar, Naga thambiran, Saniyesvarar, Bhairavar, the Sun and the Moon.

Regular pujas are observed daily and all the festivals held in Sivan temples are celebrated throughout the year. Special festival observation is made in the month of June each year.

A special re-inauguration Kumba Abishekam ceremony was held in the year 1961.

44. LANKATHEESWARAN SIVAN TEMPLE, NUWARA ELIYA

A new Sivan temple of recent origin is the Lankatheeswaran Alayam at No. 82 Lady McCallum's Drive, Nuwara Eliya, founded in 1978.

Every one is well versed in the story of the great epic 'Ramayanam'. Ravana, Lord of Lanka Pura was not only skilled in arms but was also endowed with a saintly and devoted personality. He revered Lord Siva and the object of his adoration was the Siva Lingam. It is said that he regularly performed Siva puja. Wherever he went he is said to have carried a golden Siva Lingam with him, before which, he would sing and dance in ecstasy.

By long tradition the Nuwara Eliya region, the central hill country area of Sri Lanka, has been associated with the ancient realm of Ravana. Lanka puri was his capital city. So it is of no wonder that shades of Ravana's holy worship and residual vibrations once emitted in his ecstasy and devotion is said to even now pervade Nuwara Eliya, to be felt by those capable of responding. The seer Sivabalayogi Maharaj narrates (ref 1) that Meganathan, Ravana's son, to perpetuate the memory of his father, gave merits to him, worshipping a suyambu Lingam. 'Taken up with the dedication and devotion of Meganathan, the devas led by Brahma, Vishnu, Maheswara, Indra have been hovering for ever here,' the seer had explained, ' the very same premises in which Sri Lankeswarar temple now is founded. So, it has been blessed.'

Installed in this temple we find a suyambu (shaped by itself naturally) Lingam which the eminent seer yogi, referred to above, had found after 12 years of penance by the banks of the holy river Narmada in India. He has endowed this precious gift to Sri Lanka, installing it on the 16th of October 1978, at a temple founded in premises at No. 82, Lady Maccallum's Drive. Many miracles are being attributed to this Alayam and the daily midday puja is very auspicious.

The Hindu devotees of Sri Lanka are greatly indebted to R. K. Murugesu swamy, a celebrated devotee, who has made a Siva alayam possible at this ancient locality hallowed by Ravana.

Reference:

1.   Temple booklet, 1981

ANCIENT SIVAN TEMPLES - NOW NON EXTANT

45. THIRU THAMBALESWARAM, KANTERODAI, JAFFNA

History has it that the Northern territory of this Island was at one time occupied by the Nagas. The growth of the Naga civilisation and its development may be read in Mudaliyar C. Rasanayagam's book on 'Ancient Jaffna'. The capital of the Naga kingdom in the North was Kadiramalai, near the present Kanterodai situated about five or six miles from Keerimalai. Among their places of worship was one which was later built up or restored by King Vijaya and named Thiru Thambaleswaram. It is stated (ref 1) that this temple at Thiruthampalai housed the deities Lord Thiru Thambaleswaran and Ammayar Thiru Thambaleswari. Another view (ref 2) is that Vijaya, who undoubtedly was a Hindu, built the temple Thiruthambaleswaran in the north of Ceylon. This temple must have been situated near the present Keerimalai, as there are lands in the vicinity still bearing the name of 'Thiruthampalai'. The Kadiramalai - Thiruthampalai region thus becomes a place of reverence and sanctity. Such a place would obviously be honoured, by preference, to receive the sacred Pattini Devi's relics, brought to Lanka by King Gaja Bahu. As will be read later, a magnificent edifice was erected here to venerate the Devi.

Even in subsequent history, we learn that pious monarchs revered the holy place by erecting monuments in commemoration, in the region.

As time elapsed, due to neglect and devastation, the place has gone into ruin becoming covered up, and the name Kadiramalai has also changed to Kanterodai.

Excavations at Kanterodai
Pious Monarchs revered the sacred place by erecting monuments, now revealed by excavations
commenced by Dr. Paul E. Pieris in 1912.

Exploratory investigation and excavation of an area in Kanterodai has revealed many interesting finds of archaeological interest, bearing on religious and historical events of the past.

Excavations (1917 -1919)

Dr. Paul E.Pieris first carried out excavation of some of the mounds, in the area, during 1917 - 1919. He stated his findings in two lectures delivered before the Royal Asiaic Society (Ceylon Branch), titled 'Nagadipa and the Budhist remains in Jaffna' (ref 3). A well considered judgement is revealed by him in his summary:

'It will be seen that the village of Kanterodai has no reason to be ashamed of its contribution towards the increase of our knowledge, regarding the ancient history of our Island... **I suggest that the North of Ceylon was a flourishing settlement centuries before Vijaya was born. Possibly there may have been a Siva Shrine at Thiruthampalai, as its name would suggest, which the King restored to a proper temple, rededicating it.**'

Recent Excavations

Excavation of more mounds in the area was again commenced in 1966. What were found has been described by Dr. C. E. Godekumbura in a talk (ref 4) before the R.A.S. (C.B.). The finds consisted essentially of stupas, large and small, varying in diameter from 2.6 ft. to 6 ft. Up to 1968 twenty three of them had been unearthed. Since then another thirty more have been excavated. Besides stupas the remains of a building, floors and spur stones were among the early finds.

Assessment of the probable date of the Kanterodai civilization

In this connection an interesting news item published on 02 May 1982 in the Sri Lanka newspaper 'Weekend' was that the **University of Pennsylvania had completed the evaluation of 14 radio carbon and 15 charcoal finds unearthed at Kanterodai in 1970. They have informed the Sri Lanka Archaeological Department that they were of opinion that the Kanterodai civilisation was dated by them as being of the B.C. 500-100 period, i.e., about 2500 years ago.** A piece of clay with letters and markings was also found.

References:

1.   'Yalpana Vaipava Malai', p.6

2.   Rasanayagam C. Mudaliyar, 'Ancient Jaffna', p.53

3.   J.R.A.S. (CB): Vol xxvi No. 70 pt. 1,1917, pp 11-30, vol xxviii No. 72, pt 1-4, 1919 pp 40-66

4.   J.R.A.S. (Ceylon): vol xii new series 1968, pp 67-73

46. NAVA SAILAM (NAVAKIRI), PUTTUR, JAFFNA

About twelve miles North of Jaffna, there is a 'Rock of Wonder' known by the ancients as 'Nava Sailam'. On this unique rock, elevated above ground level and about five (arm?) lengths wide, there was once a cave,

In the centre of the cave, there reigned supreme Iswara, Sankarar, with His consort Uma Devi, seated on a throne decked with blue sapphire precious stones. Sankarar, who is Vindu Nada Rupar, had Vinayaka murthi on His left and Subramaniya murthi on the right; with Nandhi Devar and Devas assembled in celestial array, he was bestowing Grace for the welfare of the devotees. When all at once, amidst the roar of thunder, the rock split asunder and there arose Mother Ganga Devi from the depths below, bubbling with marine beings and decked with lotus. Supreme Parameswaran, benign to all beings, blessed Her and placing a drop of Her waters on His braid, perpetuated the theertha waters, thus rendered sacred, for the benefit of all. This sthalam thus becomes a sacred theertham, particularly auspicious on holy days. Any one bathing in it, absolves himself of all sins. So narrates Dhakshana Kailasa Puranam - Ch. 19.

Here then is a puranic record of the evolution of one of Jaffna's landmarks. What scientific event does this depict? Whatever that may be, we have today unique features at this theertha sthalam now known as 'Nava Kiri' or 'Nilawarai' at Puttur.

There are no traces or ruins of any ancient temple at the site today. There is also a tradition (ref 1) that Sri Rama Bhagavan obtained water for his forces from here.

I became devoted to the religious sanctity of this Sthalam when in 1949 I undertook the task of a scientific examination of the contents of the much talked of 'bottomless well at Puttur' and its water resources. The findings are given in detail as the subject is of great public interest.

A simple shrine to 'Sankarar' was erected at the site to perpetuate the puranic legend of the place, thus creating a harmonious environment to my undertaking; details of what were found during the tests and the conclusions derived are narrated below:

The Nilavarai Well at Puttur

This well at Puttur appears on the surface very much like an ordinary rectangular pit or 'Kerni' as these are often called.

The water level in the kerni or well is about 0.2 ft. below mean sea level. In this respect this well hardly differs from any other well in the neighbourhood, where the surface water level is about M.S.L., but they have only 5 to 10 ft. of water.

The well is deeper on one side than it is on the other, being 134 feet on one side and 164 ft. 6 inches on the opposite side. The water level is approximately 17 feet below the average ground level in the area. This level corresponds to about 0.2 feet below Mean Sea Level Datum. The well, though approximately 48 feet by 38 feet at the water surface level, opens out to a much wider and undefinable area lower down, beneath the top land crust.

Its Formation

Puttur is about 17 feet higher than mean sea level and abounds with limestone rock. In fact, as is well known, the entire Jaffna Peninsula is a region of limestone of the Miocene age; at many places this limestone crops up to the surface and appears pitted with holes as a honey-comb mass, due to weathering; these holes and canals, when underground form ideal receptacles for subterranean storage of rain water. Thus the storing of water in the limestone becomes possible due to its own solubility. The storing up is also induced by joints and faults. The dissolving action, going on relentlessly, changes the configuration of the underground water storehouses and canalways, forming caverns. Formation of larger under-ground caverns in any particular spot cannot remain static without causing subsidences under or even on the surface. Ingress of sea water into such subsidences, caverns and cavities, when situated well below sea level, is inevitable due to the possible indefinite and innumerable number of channel links in the porous limestone. Thus it is not surprising to find fresh water at the top and salt water in the lower reaches of the Nilawarai - a deep, very deep or 'bottomless' well.

Nature of water in the well

Water in the well contained up to about 50 feet depth, is of potable quality derived from rain water draining directly into the well, having percolated through the limestone formation. From 50 ft. to 70 ft. depth, the quality of the water contained is satisfactory, though presence of dissolved impurities becomes evident. The 10 ft. column, from a depth of 70 ft. to 80 ft. from surface level, stands the layer or column of separation, between the rain derived potable water and the sea derived brackish water below. Commencing from 80 ft. depth, the quality of the water deteriorates rapidly and at about 130 ft. depth, the composition of the contents is comparable to sea water. Below the 130 ft depth, the contents are even heavier than sea water and have more dissolved solids.

The Subterranean Cavern - explored

It had become evident that the well was able to receive a fairly fast supply of sea water which apparently reached it in the zone below 50 ft. depth as the quality changed very rapidly at about 90 ft. depth. Bore holes were laid down, each 50 feet away from the well, in separate directions and drilling exploration was made utilising two steam driven percussion drills. Progress was slow but the results were striking. At the hole direct east of the well, water was struck at 20 ft. from the ground and the drilling continued but when a depth of 87 ft. was reached, there was an abrupt drop of 92 ft., indicating a cavity or possibly a cavern. At the next hole the same cavity was encountered here dropping from 81 ft. depth, by 108 feet. The southern hole indicated a cavity of 103 ft., commencing from a depth of 63 ft.

These tend to indicate the possible existence of a subterranean 100 ft. cavern (that is if all the above not be sheer coincidence) at the locality, beneath a 70 foot upper crust. It is to be considered that the ancient record found in the Sri Dhakshana Puranam, after all, be a narrative of some terrestrial phenomenon. In any case into this cavern, sea water enters and into this cavern fresh water percolates driving and pressing the heavier sea water back, until removal by pumping.

There is a local story of how a youth, to escape the long arm of the law was seen jumping into the well and was given up as drowned at the bottom of the 'bottomless' well. He only sought refuge in the cavern and came up and out into the open when his chasers had dispersed.

The celestial assembly of Lord Sankarar, and his retinue of Divines and Devas, cannot be perceived at the site today, neverthless we can witness His benign Grace bestowing flowing water for cultivation benefits of over a hundred acres, daily.

Reference:

1.   Dhakshana Kailasa Puranam, Ch. 19

47. SAMBESWARAM NEAR MATAKAL, JAFFNA
Ancient Sea Port of Sambuthurai (Jambukolam)

An ancient place of Hindu worship called Sambesvaram, housing the sacred Iswaran deity (Sambu - giver of boons), has been mentioned as having existed in Sambachurai or Sambukovalam Sea Port, built by King Thissai Maluwan in ancient Jaffna.

'In the nothern coasts of the Jaffna Peninsula' says Navaratnam (ref 1) 'to the West of Keerimalai is Sambuturai. Tradition says that it was so named because of the landing of the image of Sambu (Siva) - He who grants boons. In ancient times, Sambeswaram temple stood close to this port. In the Sinhalese Chronicles it is called Jambokola. Kovalam literally means a point jutting into the ocean; there are three of them along the northern coast: Kovalam in Karainagar, Sambukovalam to the west of Keerimalai and Kal Kovalam off Pt Pedro.

'In Ancient Lanka' Nicholas (ref 2) says 'Jambukola was the Port which envoys of Devanampiya Tissa to the Mauryan Emperor, Asoka, set sail from, as well as returned to, in the year B.C. 247'. He also adds that 'the landing of the Bodhi Tree in B.C. 246 took place at Jambukola'. This was ceremoniously brought to the Island by Princess Sangamitta. Other ports in the Jaffna Peninsula, at that time were at Valikamam and at Madduvil. These ports were less important commercially, than the international port at Matoddam, but were frequently used for travel to and from India.

Sambukovalam, an ancient sea-port on the Northern Coast

The location was blessed with another holy event when Gaja Bahu I, bearing with him the sacred symbol anklet of Pattini Kannakai Ammal, landed here in 112 AC., thereby instituting Kannakai worship in Sri Lanka. Shrines for her reverence called Kannakai Amman Kovils and Pattini Devi Devales now abound all over the Island.

There has been speculation as to the exact locality of Jambukola, in the Jaffna Peninsula. Codrington is said to have identified it as modern Sambilturai near Kankesanturai. This however is not accepted now. Navaratnam in the quotation made above states, 'a little to the east of Sambuturai (Jambukovalam) was once landed the stone image of Parvati, the consort of Siva, and from thence that place was called Matha - kal (mother as stone) and later Mathagal'; that is Matakal of today.

Raghavan (ref 3) refers to it as 'a site reputed by the name of Sambeswaram, west of Keerimalai, also known as Sambuturai.'

Sambeswaran Thiru Kovil gets mentioned in an old Tamil Composition called 'Paralai Vinayakar Pallu'. This was composed by Sinnathamby Pulavar of Nallur who lived during the days of the Dutch Regime near Saddanathar Kovil. It was first published by Sivapragasa Pandithar in 1889 and has been reprinted since then. Paralai, it is said, was situated in Chulipuram and here existed a Sivan Kovil for Sambeswaran during the days of the Tamil King Thissai Maluwan.

Sambeswaran Temple, housing the Sambu (giver of boons) Iswaran deity, in the sea port town of Sambuthurai (Jambukovalam), would have been a most revered place, figuring prominently in the ancient days, in the religious history of the Island.

Reference:

1.   Navaratnam, C. S., 'A Short History of Hinduism in Ceylon', 1964, p. 61

2.   Nicholas, C. W., 'Historical Topography of Ancient and Medieval Ceylon', Special number, Vol. VI (1959) of the R.A.S. (C.B.), p. 83

3.   Raghavan, M.D., 'Tamil Culture in Ceylon', p. 239

48. PALINAGARAM SIVAN KOVIL RUINS, TUNUKAI

In the year 1889, Hugh Neville, the Assistant Government Agent, Mullaitivu, in the northern part of the island came across the ruins of a temple, while inspecting an old irrigation tank. The entries (ref 1) on his diary dated June 8, 1889 contain a description of what was seen by him: 'a small stone spill led to the Kovil Kadu or Temple Forest'. He has been going into the area known as Kovil Kadu situated about a mile, below the spill works of ancient Vavunikulam near Tunukai. There he saw 'the ruined temple - a large temple with its posts all fallen and its Saivaite Lingam broken'.

Vavunikulam, below which the ruins were found, is an ancient work of the pre-Christian era, known as Palivavi. The reservoir is formed by damming the flow of the river Pali-Aru, in the Tunukai District, for the development of lands in the Punakary region. Henry Parker, Engineer and Scholar, of 'Ancient Ceylon' (1909) fame, visited the place; he writes (ref 2):

The construction of Vavunikkulam, a reservoir in the Northern Province should probably be assigned to nearly the same period. Its original name was Peli-vapi, so called because it was formed by raising a long embarkment across the valley of a stream now termed the Pali River. The single reference to it in the Mahavamsa (i.p. 107) shows that it was in existence before the time of Duttha-Gamini, and this may carry its construction back to before the third century B.C.'

Therefore, there remains the possibility that it was formed during the reign of Elara (Ellalan), and that the early annalists omitted to record the fact.

Further he continues:

The reference to it in history is as follows: To northward of the capital, at the distance of seven yojanas, in the sand banks of the stream flowing into the tank of Pelivapigama, four superb gems, in size about a small grindstone and of the colour of the Umma flower, were produced. The name, the distance from the city, and the reference to a stream with sand-banks render the identification certain, there being no other reservoir on the river, and no other stream with sandbanks at that distance north of Anuradhapura ...'

It has become evident that the city of Palinagaram was known to ancient history of the first century A.D., from the references made in the rock inscription found at Perumiyankulam.

Parker made a critical study of the technical aspects of the work, comparing them with those of the well known reservoirs erected during the times of the Sinhalese Kings, pointing out the differences and concludes with the sentence. 'This variation from later practice indicates the early date of the works.'

The reference in the above, to the possibility of the work to have been formed by Ellalan, is because, as Pathmanathan writes (ref 3): 'In the second century B.C. Elara (Ellalan), a nobleman from the Cola country, subdued the Sinhalese ruler Asela and administered a large part of the island from Anuradhapura for a period of forty-four years. Early historical traditions of the Sinhalese represent him as a great and just ruler'. He came from a country where cultivation by irrigation and religious Hindu worship prevailed in a large scale and as such, is more than likely to have founded storage reservoirs and Hindu temples.

The broken Avudaiyar of Siva Lingam found at Kovil Kadu appears of a much older period than the upright Rudra Paham. They may be from two different cultural eras.

Historically, centuries later, this region, along with the neighbourhood, was developed during the regime of the Vanni chiefs - the era of glory of the Vanni. During such a period, any work such as Vavunikulam and the Sivan Temple situated in Pali-Nagaram would have been improved and maintained.

Hence, it was not surprising to find remnants of ruins of two distinct eras of civilisation and development here.

Pali Nagaram was complete with its Sivan Temple, water reservoir and a large suburban settlement many of which exist today, such as Panan Kamam, Manner Kulam, Thattan Kulam, Vanankamam, and Nagapaduvankulam. At the tail end of the scheme, close to the sea, was Pu-Nagaram, the Punakari of today.

Remnants of two separate eras of development were distinctly discernable when I first visited the location in 1940. The tank, then lying breached and abandoned in thick jungle showed an ancient goose-neck spill which had later been supplanted by a masonry right bank spill prevalent during the medieval period. At the temple site, the broken Avudaiyar of the Siva Lingam was of a much older period compared to the upright portion (also broken) seen at the site.

This is the story of an ancient Hindu place of worship, a Siva Sthalam, situated in the area called by the villagers as Kovil Kadu, below Vavunikulam in Tunukai, off Mankulam.

References:

1. Brohier, 'Ancient Irrigation Works', Part II, p. 15

2. Ceylon Govt Sessional paper XLVIII of 1886 - Report by Henry Parker

3. Pathmanathan, S., 'The Kingdom of Jaffna', 1978 - p. 19

49. SANDIRASEKARAN KOVIL, CHEDDIKULAM

About fifteen miles from Madawachchi on the road to Mannar may be found a small and not so well maintained shrine, dedicated to the worship of Vinayaka Murthi. The site and the tank, across the road, known as Muhattan Kulam mark the turn off for an ancient holy site, situated at Vavvalai, about four miles interior to the South.

The 'Manual of the Vanni' by J. P. Lewis (1895) (ref 1) has the following: 'The Division of Cheddikulam is said to have been colonized in the Kaliyuga 3348 (about 247 AC.) by a chetty from Madura, who with some Parava pearl fishers had been wrecked on the coast of Ceylon. This is the account given of it: 'Vira Narayana Cheddi came to Adankapattu, settled in Cheddikulam, built or dug the kerni called Vavvalai, and erected a temple to Santirasekeran. He buried in a well near the temple treasure which it took sixty elephants to carry, and left a devil-chadamuni, to watch it, and local tradition has it, that this treasure will be revealed by the 'muni' who is guarding it, to any one who rebuilds the temple that was destroyed by the Portuguese'. Not much else is known about this temple of the third century.

It cannot now be rebuilt at the original site near Vavvalai lake as that area will get submerged by the proposed Malwattu Reservoir.

Reference:

1.   Lewis J. P. 'The Manual of the Vanni', 1895

50. TONDESWARAM NEAR MANTOTA

An ancient Siva Sthalam mentioned by the well known historian Dr. Paul E. Pieris in his writings is Tondeswaram. He writes (ref 1): (to repeat the quotation, appearing already).

'Long before the arrival of Vijaya, there were in Lanka five recognised Iswarams of Siva which claimed and received adoration of all India. These were Tiruketheeswaram near Mahatittha, Munneswaram dominating Salawatta and the pearl fishery, Tondeswaram near Mantota, Tirukoneswaram near the great Bay of Kottiyar and Naguleswaram near Kankesanturai.

'Their situation close to those ports cannot be the result of accident or caprice, and was probably determined by the concourse of a wealthy mercantile population whose religious wants called for attention.'

The Yalpana Vaipava Malai (ref 2) mentions the same event and activity. It describes how King Vijayan safeguarded his small island kingdom with four (Siva) Iswaran temples, situated in the four different directions of Lanka. The Konesar temples at Thampalakamam to the East, Thiruketheeswaram Temple at Matoddam to the West, Thiru Thambaleswaram Temple at Keerimalai to the North and Sandirasekeran Temple at Matara. What has been referred to as 'Tondeswaram near Mantota' by Dr. P. E. Pieris may be a temple other than Thiruketheeswaram at Matoddam. The four temples are referred to by Dr. C. Sivaratnam (ref 3): 'Vijaya himself was a Saivaite who built Siva alayams in the four quarters of Ceylon for protection of his infant Kingdom'.

Tondeswaram remains to be identified.

Reference:

1.   Pieris, Paul E., J.R.A.S. (C.B.) Vol. xxvi No. 70, pp 17-18

2.   Yalpana Vaipava Malai 1953 Edition, p. 6 (original: Mailvakanapulavar of Mathakal, Jaffna, 1736)

3.   Sivaratnam Dr. C, 'The Tamils in early Ceylon'

51. RAJARAJESWARAM IN MATODDAM, MANNAR

The Chola power lasted two centuries in India, but they held sway over Lanka only from 1017 to 1070 A. C, they were devout Saivaites and building of places of Hindu worship, and that too in stone masonry architecture, had been a characteristic feature of their regime.

Matoddam was an important Chola stronghold in Sri Lanka, others being Polannaruwa, Padaviya and Trincomalee. It was the Island's chief sea-port and being close to South India, served as a landing place.

Chola inscriptions from Mantai have provided us valuable information about the temples erected by them at Matoddam. Dr. S. Pathmanathan of the University of Jaffna, who has studied these, has contributed a most valuable article about them to a Thiruketheeswaram Temple publication (ref 1) of 1976, from which, what follows has been collected:

Three Chola inscriptions were discovered at Thiruketheeswaram some time back and their contents have been deciphered and published in Vol. IV of South Indian Inscriptions as Nos. 1412 and 1414.

These inscriptions provide information about Rajarajeswaram and Tiruviramisvaram (vide Ch. 23) which are two temples erected by them at Matoddam. Presumably they were at Thiruketheeswaram itself, where the inscriptions were found.

Rajarajeswaram was named after the great Chola ruler Rajaraja Cholan. Many consider that the ancient Siva Sthalam Thiruketheeswaram, itself, may have been restored and renamed Rajarajeswaram by the Cholas. It was erected by Talikumaran who came from Cirukurranallur in Velar Nadu and who must have held a very high and responsible position at Matoddam. He made provision for the maintenance of the temple he had erected by making endowments of land and government revenue for conducting daily rituals and festivals and the water-cutting ceremony, during the seven day festivals finishing with Vishakam in the month of Vaikasi, annually.

The Inscriptions

Dr. S. Pathmanathan writes 'The first of these, which refers to the construction of Rajarajeswaram at Matoddam by Tali Kumaran, a Chola official, is inscribed on all the four sides of a pillar which is 4' 5' x 8' in dimension. Some lines of writing at the beginning and end of each side of the pillar were found to have been completely obliterated. In its present state of preservation the epigraph has ninety eight lines of writing... it could be assigned to the early eleventh century on palaeographical considerations and the basis of its contents...' most of the details recorded in this inscription are not to be found in any other source.'

TRANSLATION

The lands (including five rods measured by ... kot to the north and) having the blacksmith's quarter in the north, the Rajarajapperucteru on the west, ... as its four great boundaries with the exclusion of the houses, mansion and garden of Kunran Kaman, - an inhabitant of this town - have been given as tax free deva dana, to last as long as the sun and the moon endure, to Rajarajeswaram which has been erected at Matottan otherwise called Rajarajapuram in Ceylon otherwise called Mummudi Colamandalam by Talikumaran, the chief of Cirukur-ranallur of Velar nadu in Ksatriya sikhamani valanadu in Colamandalam.

Let him contribute daily two vaddam from the amount collected as tolls from the pathways leading to arumalitteva valanadu otherwise called... naikkoti nadu and also the pidilikai vari. From the income derived from the looms in the town, from the vaddam and from the pathways and ferries rituals, festivals and the water-cutting ceremony shall be performed for the seven days of Vicakam in the month of Vaikaci (at this temple).

Money shall be collected at the rate of an akham (per day?) for transport through pathways and ferries. A monthly levy shall be made on all weavers in this town at the rate of one-eigth of an akkam per loom. A levy shall be made on all commercial transactions at the rate of a vattam per kasu on all buyers and sellers. From the proceeds of the amount thus collected provision shall be made for supplying daily six measures of rice for the offering of three sacred meals, eight measures of paddy for two young Brahmins and ... for a chief of the Matam (inn)... .

Reference:

1.   Pathmanathan, Dr. S., 'Chola Inscriptions from Mantai' in Thiruketheeswaram Thirukuda - thiru manjana Malar, 1976, pp 59-70

52. THIRUVIRAMISVARAM, MATODDAM, MANNAR

Like Rajarajeswaram, Thiruviramisvaram also was a place of Hindu worship erected by the Cholas at Matoddam, information about which came to light as a result of the inscriptions found at Thiruketheeswaram, some time back. These inscriptions have been described earlier. The particular inscription related to this temple 'records the grant made to the temple of Tiruviramisvaram by an official of Rajendra. Besides, it mentions some communities of Tamil traders who were settled in the neighbourhood of the temple' (ref 1).

The title 'Thiru-vi-Ramisvaram' recalls the name of the celebrated sthalam Rameswaram, on the other side of Palk Strait. The inscription records 'the gift of four gold coins for burning lamps daily at this shrine'. Two of the coins were deposited with the 'Canharapadiyar' living in Matoddam. The third and the fourth coins were deposited with the Valakkay Vaniyar and the Verilli Vaniyar also of Matoddam.

Translation of Inscription:

'Hail! Prosperity!... Tevan Cantiman, the Utaiyan of Cirukulattur, serving Rajendra Devar in the capacity of a member of the (military) group of Peruntanam has deposited two kasus with the Cankarapadiyar of the town (Matottam), one kasu with the Verrilai Vaniyar of the town and another kasu with the Valakkay Vaniyar of the same town as an endowment for the temple called Tiruviramisvaram at Matottam otherwise called Rajarajapuram (sanctified by the consecration of the image of Iksvakutevar in the temple of the Great Lord of Tiruviramisvaram). With the income from the four kasus thus deposited (lamps called cantivilakku' shall be lighted).

As a matter of interest, it is cogent to speculate on the precise location of the two temples the Cholas erected at Matoddam. Rajarajeswaram, as has been mentioned earlier, has been identified by some as being Thiruketheeswaram Temple itself. The second shrine Tiruviramisvaram was probably an additional temple of later erection. Searching for references in later documents, there are two of interest. These apparently refer to sites closer to the junction of main Mannar - Punakari Road and the temple approach road. Sir William Twynam, the Government Agent, in his inspection notes refers to the possibility of a temple having existed near about the site of the old Mantai Rest House. In this connection, the Government Agent's Diary entry dated 22nd May, may be read in the Administration Report of the Northern Province for the year 1887.

The building of the old Mantai Rest House may well have been the structure found there today, which serves as Government Quarters.

Reference:

1.   Pathmanathan, Dr. S., 'Chola Inscriptions from Mantai', in Thiruketheeswaram Thirukuda-thiru Manjana Malar, 1976 pp. 59-70

53. SIVAN KOVIL RUINS, KACHCHILAMADU
Near Pandara Vanniyan Memorial

In the hinterland, off Oddichuddan about fifteen miles from Mullaitivu, are found ruins of an ancient Sivan temple. The location derives its name from the fact that a stone monument had been erected there, in memory of a valliant Vanni Chief named Pandara Vanniyan.

Kachchilamadu Memorial Stone commemorating the site where valiant Pandara Vanniyan fell
Remnants of old Sivan Kovil are near by

The heroic episode of Pandara Vanniyan is well known to every household in the Vanni District. He is said to have resisted all attempts by the foreign invaders to subdue him and the Vanni regime. His eventual fall due to encirclement from many directions is well remembered by the Vanni folks.

The memorial stone monument found today at the spot where he fell is said to have been a tribute to his valour by his opponants. Hence the name 'Kachchila - madu', meaning the place where there is a memorial stone.

Not much is known about the temple, the remnants of which are found today at the site. It probably was his temple of solace and where he retreated when demise threatened him.

SECTION III

MURUGAN TEMPLES

54. VENERATION OF MURUGAN

The origin of Murugan and the story of his veneration are of very ancient interest. The story is fundamental in the history of development of Tamil Culture. He becomes identified as 'Kumaran' - the adolescent, 'Skanda' the seed that was produced, 'Karthikeya' - nurtured by the constellation Pleiades (Kartikai), 'Velan' the lance bearer, 'Subrahmaniya' - the supreme Brahman and also as the Leader of the Celestials. His name has been revered as a Divine from antiquity. Through the ages his name has been cherished as the Patron Deity of the Tamil Race and the Tamil Language.

In Ancient Tamil Literature

The pre-Aryan pre-historic eras are known to have revered a rudimentary form of Murugan, a youth of valorous deeds who was victorious in war and in hunting.

The earliest Tamil literary works known are the compositions of the Tamil Sangam (or academy) eras. These have been collected and published today as anthologies, titled 'Ettu tokai' or eight anthologies, and 'Pathu Paadal' or the Ten Idylls. Scholars have dated these as being of the first and the third centuries.

Of these, three works concern us. They are 'Paripadal' and 'Kalitokai' of the early Ettu thokai anthologies and the 'Thiru-muru-katru-padai', the last of the Pathu Paadal lyrics.

Several references appear in these to a Murugan. The hill country was his domain and he was the lord of the hunt. His name was associated with the leadership of the Kurunchi tracts in the country. He also gets referred to as 'Ceyon' the 'red one'. The elephant was one of his pet animals. He rode on the peacock as his steed, carrying a banner with a cock emblem and with a leaf shaped spear or lance. Could this Chief or Leader eventually become venerated as 'Kadavul' or deity?

The Pandiyans accepted him as a Divine and paid reverance. Figuring persistantly ever afterwards in Tamil Literature, he becomes upheld today as the source and inspiration of the Tamil Language and the Tamil People.

Birth

The Puranas extol his legendary origin. The Devas, when they proceeded to Mount Kailas to complain to Lord Siva of their persecution by the Asuras, found him in deep meditation. On being awakened, a Divine spark emanated from his frontal third eye. This was received in Lake Saravana Poikai. There it was nurtured by the constellation Pleiades (Karthikai) and became six infants. They became one when they were fondly embraced by Divine Mother-Gooddess Parvathi. Therefore he is also known as Karthikeya. This miraculous origin is treasured in the Puranas with the much cherished verse:

'That which was formless, became a Form, a column of light, the Brahmam,
the one, the many, the Endless,
became One Body:
Six faces abundant with Grace;
twelve mighty arms; one thiru Murugan
arose and arrived
for the world to be saved'.

Kandapuranam I (II)

Murugan as a valourous youth is said to have performed several brave deeds including the imprisonment of Brahma and imparting the meaning of the sacred word AUM to Lord Siva. In due course he was sent, accompanied by a large force, with Virapahu at the Head, to overcome the Asuras and release the Devas.

A preliminary event in this episode was the confrontation with Tharaka, the Lion faced brother of the Asura leader. Tharaka when challenged sought refuge in Mount Kraunchi, which emitted fire and smoke. It was blown up into pieces by missiles from Murugan. Legends have it that when it broke up splinters were flung far and wide. Three places where some of the splinters are said to fallen, in Sri Lanka are Thirukovil, Mandur and Okanda hill top; these places have much cherished Muruga Sthalams today.

Before the actual commencement of the battle, Veerapahu was sent as an emissary to Mahentrapura, the citadal of the Asuras; he however failed to persuade Surapadman to lay down arms or release the Devas. On the first day of the battle Bhanukopan, the eldest son of the Asura chief, who offered combat, was overcome. Then the lion faced Singamukan, a brother of Surapadman, who came to his aid, was defeated. Upon which the Asura Leader himself fought, assuming several monstrous forms and shapes; finally he sought refuge in the form of a mango tree. He was ultimately defeated but was not slain but accepted to serve Muruga as his steed in the form of a peacock and also given a place in his banner as a rooster cock. The Devas were released and they celebrated the victory.

His Consorts

Indra the King of the Devas and Indrani, his Queen, rewarded Murugan by giving him their daughter Deiva Yanai or Deivanai (borne by the celestial elephant) also called Deva Sena (The Divine Army), in marriage. The grand nuptial celebrations are claimed to have taken place at Thiruperumkunram situated a few miles from Madurai.

Murugan's second consort is Valli, the Veddah maid, from the Vallimalai hills. Veddah chief Nambi found her as an infant in the jungles and brought her up. Valli, literally, is the name of an entwining creeper. She grew up as a devotee of Murukan. Eventually Murukan wins her hand and she is given in marriage to him. The event itself is an interesting episode. Kataragama, a village in the South of Sri Lanka is associated by many as being the scene of this episode. Today the shrine there is very highly venerated.

The Vel

A leaf shaped spear was from early days the weapon of the hunter. It became Murugan's weapon for overcoming evil forces, thus becoming a symbol of Power, a power to punish evil. In due course it became a symbol of spiritual victory. Devotees venerate the VEL today as representing Murugan himself. Puranas extol the ceremonial bestowment of the Vel by the Divine Mother to Lord Murugan.

In a philosophical interpretation, the two consorts are considered to represent Kiriya Sakthi and Ichcha Sakthi; and the Vel or the Lance his power of will or Jnana Sakthi. His overpowering the indestructible Asura Leader and transforming him as a steed to ride on is symbolic that natural forces cannot be destroyed, even when they are against Gods. They of course could be overcome and made to serve instead.

Tiru murukatru padai

Thirumurukatrupadai is a Tamil poem of antiquity composed by the venerable Poet Nakkirar, on the veneration of Murugan. It is the earliest Tamil composition known and has been dated as belonging to the second century. While on a pilgrimage to Kasi, Nakkirar was seized by goblins and confined in a cave. There he composed this celebrated work extolling the powers and the Grace of Murugan, for the benefit of his fellow captives. The work, besides being a treasure of Tamil literature of the period, is a sacred and ritual prayer invoking Murugan to their aid. Murugan's Grace enabled them to regain their liberty.

The Poem also enumerates six places as being especially auspicious for his veneration. They are well known Muruga Sthalams today and are visited by every Muruga devotee:-

1.   Thiruperumkunram, about 5 miles S.W. of Madurai in South India, where his wedding ceremony with Deivanai is believed to have taken place.

2.   Thiruchendur on the south-east coast of India, which commemorates his overpowering the Asuras.

3.   Palani where Murugan retreated as an ascetic.

4.   Swami malai where he is said to have initiated Lord Siva.

5.   Alagar Cholai or Palamutir Cholai, about 13 miles from Madurai. Nowadays the hillock Thiruthanni is fast gaining over this place.

6.   It is sung that Murugan sports about on every Hill, so all hill tops are enumerated for the sixth Place. Some refer to the Kataragama peak in Sri Lanka as the sixth sacred place of Murugan.

In Sri Lanka the Muruga temples at the following places viz: at Kataragama in South Lanka, Nallur at Jaffna, Selva-Sannithy near Valvettithurai, Maviddapuram near

Kankesanthurai, Mandur in Batticaloa, Sithandi also near Batticaloa may be cited as being among the six prominent Muruga Sthalams today.

References

1.   Clothey Fred, W. 'The Many Faces of Murugan', Mouton Publishers, 1978

2.   Zvelebil Kamil, V. 'A guide to Murugan' in the Journal of Tamil Studies of the I.I.T.S.

55. NALLUR KANDASWAMY TEMPLE, JAFFNA

Nallur is my birth place and all my early years were spent in and around this temple. The temple and its festivals hold a commanding influence on me. Along with others, we were a band of youths who spent days attending to the various chores needed for a temple to function, all of which are now attended to by paid employees. I can well remember the several occasions when we fell foul with 'the visaran' the mad fellow, who had his unauthorised abode in the 'ther muddi' or the place where the ratham was parked. He would resent our breaking into his hideout to take out the ratham ropes for airing and cleaning. Little did we realise then, that we were the companions (though often scolded miserably) of a sage and savant Chellapah Swamy, now revered as the Guru of Yoga Swamykal. His guttural voice announcing in never ending strains that 'no harm was intended to anyone', 'it had already happened' - still rings in my ears.

The Nallur Kandaswamy Temple, Jaffna

The Nallur Kandaswamy temple is not very ancient; its origin is known to history; there are several publications on the subject. According to the 'Yalpana Vaipava Malai' the origin is attributed to Bhuvenaka-Vaku, Chief Minister to Kulangai Ariya Chakravarti, who was reigning at Singai Nagar. However, several references give the entire credit for building the city of Nallur and the Kandaswamy Temple to Sempaha Perumal who ruled at Nallur under the name of Bhuvenka Bahu for 17 years from 1450 AC. He of course may have been responsible for the erection of a proper structure ot traditional temple status, restoring an earlier structure in the city that he had demolished in the course of warfare; whoever it may be, the 'Katiyam' recitals of the temple today name the founder of the temple as a Bhuvaneka Vaku.

The structure was the pride of Jaffna; it was not at the present site but at 'Sangili Thoppu', about half a mile to the east, where are found the ruins of the palace complex of the Nallur kings. We read, that (ref 1) 'the famous Tamil king got down 'Thirtham' water in 'kavadis' from the Yamuna and deposited it in an 'Eri' (pond) dug out for this purpose near the present Nallur Christian Church. This pond is still there and is known as Yamuneri. The other historical places round about Sangilithoppu are Pandaramallikai, Pandaram-padda-Valavu and Rajavinthodam. The temple was levelled to the ground in 1620 by Philip de Oliveira, after Sangili Kumara's defeat in the battle of Vannarponnai, leaving no traces of its foundation.'

The present Kandaswamy temple at Nallur originated during the days of the Dutch rule, when, in 1749, Ragunatha Mappana Mudaliyar who was in the service of the Dutch Government and enjoyed their favour, got their permission to use a madam for holding Kandapuranam recitals; it later became a temple and eventually a proper temple structure was erected in 1807 by the Mudaliyar, who was then Shroff at the Jaffna Kachcheri.

Arumuga Navalar took a great interest in the temple, during the years 1870 et seq. His insistence on the temple rituals being performed in accordance with traditional ways often brought him in conflict with the management. In any case, he is said to have been responsible for installing the principal deity in the correct place, for introducing group recitals of thevarams after the puja, and the discontinuance of sacrifice of animals and nautch dance performances.

Lately, several additions and improvements have been made to the temple structure by the efficient management in charge. A well built Raja Gopuram and two other Gopurams were early additions. The inner southern praharam was rebuilt widening it and a Gopuram erected over the Arumuga Swamy entrance. Among the very recent modifications are changes in the frontal portals, widening and ornating it with artistic sculptural pillars. The trustees are descendants of Ragunatha Mappana Mudaliyar.

The daily puja ceremonies are performed meticulously and punctualy, at the stipulated times, correct to the minute. Large numbers of devotees attend the daily pujas; the morning and the evening pujas are particularly well attended. In addition special puja ceremonies and festivals are held on most of the days. Karthikai and Sashdi days of the month are devoted to special festivals. The commencing day of each month is noted by a theertha festival. The reading of the sacred Kantha Puranam, being a narrative of the Sri Murukan story commences in April and goes on terminating with the Suran Por festival in October. There is said to be a special occasion on almost every day of the week.

The annual festival is a stupendous grand occasion, lasting twenty-six days, finishing on the new moon day in August. This festival commences with the flag hoisting ceremonies on the first day, sharp at 12 noon, and two festivals are conducted daily ; the Peacock and Annam Vahanams are used in the mornings and in the evening, the vahanams are varied. On the tenth day, the Kailasa Vahanam is used in the morning. In the evening the Muthu Cumaraswamy Moorthy is taken out on the Manjam ratham. The Karthikai day festival, which falls on the 17th or the 18th day, the same deity is taken out on a sapparam decked with flowers and Ola leaves. The Kailasa Vahanam used on one of these days depicts Ravana carrying the entire Kailash mounted on his shoulders. On the 22nd day (Mampalam festival), the puranic immortal incident of the divine brothers Vinayakamoorthy and Sri Murugan vying for the single mango from the Parents, is depicted. We see the Thandayutha Moorthy going empty handed and Vinayakar with a mango in His hands at the end of the festival. The mammoth 'saparam' is assembled for use on the 23rd festival.

The Ther festival on the 24th day is undoubtedly the grand climax of all festivals in Jaffna. The largest crowd possible throngs the site, when Arumuga Peruman is taken out for the circumlocution at 8 am in the morning. It is truly a grand occasion which no one would forget. Religious fervour reaches peak level with the huge crowd present. The theertha festival is observed on the following day in the Thirukulam, and rituals performed for terminating the festival season, by bringing down the flag that was hoisted, at the end of the evening festival. My mother would never allow me to attend this, because the evil spirits and harmful beings that were held captive and under restraint at the Kodi Sthampam, would be released free when the flag is lowered. A divine social nuptial is depicted on the following day when the wedding of Murugan to Sri Valli is solemnised.

Arrangements for all these festive occasions require untiring organising and efficient management. Truly it is the best administered Hindu temple in the Island today. A special daily festure is the innumerable abishekams performed by devotees, so much so, that the deity at Nallur Kandaswamy temple is often referred to as ' Abisheka Murukan '.

The Statue of Sangili at Nallur

Nallur City

Nallur, the celebrated city founded by Singai Ariyan (Kulangai), the first Ariyachakravarti King of Jaffna, continued to be the capital of the several Ariya Charkravarthy Kings ruling in Jaffna as Sekarajasekaram or Pararajesekaram, for about 300 years.

The fall of Nallur commenced with the decline of the Sangili Sekarajasekaram regime (1519-1560). Today we see the ruins of the gateway to the Kings Palace, a building said to have been the residence of an important personage, and the Yamunari Theertham. A recently erected statue of Sangili reminds us to pay reverence to the original Nallur Kandaswamy Temple of Sempaha Perumal.

References:

1.   C. Sivaratnam, 'The Tamils in early Ceylon ', 1968 p. 134

56. MAVIDDAPURAM KANDASWAMY TEMPLE, KANKESANTURAI (KOVIT KADAVAI)

Kovit Kadavai, the original name of the Mavaddapuram region, is ten miles from Jaffna; it forms with Naguleswaram (Keerimalai) and Kasathurai (Kankesanturai), a celebrated triangular region of ancient name and fame.

Thither was directed Marutha Piravika Valli, daughter of Thissai Ukkira Cholan (a king of the Chola regime in South India). She was afflicted with a congenital disease which affected her facial appearance. All medical treatment had failed and she betook to pilgrimage to sacred sthalams. Sage Shanthi Linga Munivar, pitying her plight, advised her to proceed to Keerimalai, where the Lord of Naguleswaram was presiding and to perform daily theertham in the sacred fresh water spring there. Upon which Maruthappira Valli, arrived at Kovit Kadavai with her retinue of escorts and maids in attendance and took residence in proximity to the sthalam, at a locality which even today is referred to as Kumarathi Pallam. Her daily obeisance and the curative value of the medicinal waters of the fresh water spring gradually helped her to rid of the facial horse-like affliction. In her journeys to the sthalam, she had noticed an old man by the name of Sadaiyanar venerating with daily pujas a silver Vel, the emblem of God Skanda Kumaran, placed in a cove on a mango tree. She felt the divine urge to build a proper temple for housing the deity and informed her father of her desire. Very soon sthapathy architects and craftsmen arrived from Chola Nadu and commenced erecting a Kandaswamy Temple. Maruthapiravika Valli also married Ukkira Singan, a Kalinga King (8th century) of Kadiramalai (Kantarodai) Jaffna, who asked for her hand. The Skanda Vigrakam 'Kankeyan' was brought from India and landed at Kasaturai (consequently that place assumed today's name of Kankesanturai). It was installed with proper Kumba Abishekam ceremonies on an uthiram day in the ninth century. Priests and others, who also came from India, looked after the affairs of the temple and maintained it to a high standard. The place also changed its name from Kovit Kadavai to Maviddapuram (Ma=Horse).

Bhuvenga Bahu (1450 - 1467) of Nallur fame, King of Jaffna, who visited Maviddapuram, is recorded as having gone into raptures at his reception at this place.

Like all Hindu temples, this temple also suffered demolition in the hands of the foreigners in the seventeenth century, and even the stones, it is said, were removed to build the sea-fort at Kayts.

With the resuscitation of Hinduism rebuilding the temple was commenced in the year 1782. Several of the vigrakams that were hidden in wells, were recovered and the temple started functioning once more. The Kurukkal priests who assumed charge have maintained the temple and its functions to a high standard. Several improvements were done; the imposing Raja Gopuram by the Road side in the Western praharam is an outstanding contribution in which are depicted events in the history of the temple. The inner temple premises were rebuilt in heavy granite stone in 1927. A Ther of exquisite workmanship was made in 1943; a temple for Palani Andavar was added in 1964. In 1965 a new feature - the therppa thiruvila, was introduced on the last day, to the 27 day annual festivals, held in July - August. On this day the deity is taken in procession for theertham at Kankesanturai, to re-live memories of the days of Kovit Kadavai and Kasaturai. This however has been terminated now.

Reference:

1.   Ra Sunthararaja Sarma, 'Kovit Kadavai' (Tamil) 1966

2.   C S Navaratnam, 'A Short History of Hinduism', 1964.

3.   Yalpana Vaipava Malai

57. SELVA SANNITHY MURUGAN TEMPLE, THONDAIMANAR

It is revered as Sella Kadirkamam of the North, this temple for Sri Murugan at Thondaimanar, about 20 miles North of Jaffna. Here too, as at Kadirkamam, a free environment for worship pervades the place. Persons of various creeds and castes congregate here for darisanam of the Muruga Vel, installed at this blessed Sannithanam (Selva Sannithy).

The origin of this temple, which is not so very ancient, is known to history. The waters of Thondaimanar (a theertham where fresh water flows into the sea) past the site, elevates the location to a sthalam, blessed with the triple adjuncts of theertham, sthalam and moorthy. This was a water way, said to have been excavated under the supervision of Karunakara Thondaiman. He was sent here for procurement of salt supplies, by Kulathunga Cholan, who reigned in South India from 1070 to 1118 AC. The temple by the side of the newly cut water-way would have been the place of worship of the settlement that was founded in the locality. The temple however suffered the fate of devastation, like all other Hindu temples, in the hands of the foreigners of the 16th century. Later, during the era of revival of Hinduism in Jaffna, a temple was erected at the site, but differences among the management hindered its proper function.

At this stage, the story shifts to one Kadirkamar, a keen devotee of Murugan, who proceeded bewailing to Kadirkamam, and was rewarded there with the gift of a silver Vel, the emblem of Murugan. He brought this sacred Vel and installing it in a madam at the site, performed daily pujas to it. Later, he was permitted to use the temple itself, which he took over and he and his group have been managing and officiating ever since, with piety and satisfaction to all devotees.

Today, the Selva Sannithy Muruga Shrine is a well established institution, with a grand temple and several madams, in the locality. Daily hundreds of devotees and mendicants throng the place. The historical Thondaimanar Lagoon enhances the sthalam with theertham facilities and there is always food available in some madam or other in the locality, for the mendicants. Several devotees come here and distribute food - annathanam, fulfilling their vows for favours received from Him. It has become a place noted for this, so much so, that the deity Himself is known as Annathana Murugan.

The temple functions well with regular pujas and annual festivals. There is of course less ritual in the puja and other ceremonies, than are seen at temples officiated by Brahmin priests.

The construction of a salt water prevention barrage, across Thondaimanar at the site, enabled me to bow in worship at the shrine on several occasions.

Reference:

Valvai Vaithiyalingam Pillai (1852-1901) has composed a tribute to Sri Murugan titled 'Selva Sannithi Murai' (Tamil).

58. CHITRA VELAUTHA SWAMY KOVIL, KUMARAPURAM, MULLAITIVU

Off Mulliyavalai, a village few miles West of Mullaitivu is a small shrine dedicated to the worship of Skanda, called 'Chitra Velautha Swamy Kovil.' The shrine had been reasonably well maintained and was an attractive ancient structure when I first visited it in the year 1939 to pay homage to Velautha Moorthy Several devotees used to gather there, particularly on Fridays, for tharisanam of Kumarapuram Murugan.

In general, the origin of most of the Chitra Velautha Temples is to be found among the Veddah places of worship of old. Mention is made in this compilation of similar temples along the eastern coastal region to be found at Thirukovil and at Verugal. The Veddah huntsmen worship Skanda or Velautham (lance) in a simple shrine made up of sticks and leaves, which gradually becomes a place of regular worship. Such places had been built up as permanent temples during the Vanni regime. Whatever that may have been, we know that this was a temple built by the Vanni Chiefs. Stories are told in local publications, of the days of glory of this temple at a time when the rulers of the Vanni were in great power. Apparently it was in the hands of a particular 'Vanni Kudumbam', whose fortunes gradually diminished with time. The temple also became neglected.

Surprisingly this temple had escaped the notice of the foreign powers, which went about demolishing Hindu temples in the seventeenth century, may be because of its interior location and also of its non-attractive condition then.

Subsequently however, as Navaratnam says in his 'Short History of Hinduism', 'Kumarapuram was lucky to have had a line of devoted priests to carry on the services of the temple and to look after its properties'.

Kumarapuram today requires the active interest of many Muruga devotees to restore it to its former glory.

59. CHITRA VELAUTHA SWAMY KOVIL, VERUGAL, TRINCOMALEE

There exists at Kiliveddi by the banks of the Verugal Aru (a branch of the Mahaweli Ganga), a Murugan Shrine.

Kiliveddi is halfway on the road from Trincomalee to Batticaloa. It is an important landmark and halting place for the many pilgrims who go on foot from Jaffna passing Vaththapalai and Koneswaram on to Kadirgamam. The Verugal Chitra Velautha Swamy Kovil is a temple of ancient lore with a fascinating history.

A celebrated history of Trincomalee of old, has been published by V. Akilesapillai in the eighteen eighties; he has a chapter about this temple, in his work 'Tiru Konesala Vaipavam ', 1889. A more comprehensive and scholarly article entitled 'Arul Surukum Verugalam Pathy' (Tamil) is found in the 'Tiru Konesar Kumba-Abisheka Malar' contributed by S. Kanapathipillai (Lecturer).

Like all ancient shrines and temples, the origin of Verugalam Pathy Muruga Vel is also legendary. During the epoch wars of Skanda with Asura King, Sura Pathman, a dart from Skanda's sacred bow had fallen at a place now called 'Kadira Veli'. The Veddah tribes treasured it for worship, and ever since there has been this shrine, which had become a recognised temple during the Kulakoddan era and the regime of the Vanniyars.

The story of how a Nallainatha Chettiyar came to build this temple later is faithfully recorded in local tradition. The Chettiyar, a merchant from Tirunelvely in South India, was making his pilgrimage to Kadirkamam, through Trincomalee, when he stopped for a night at Verugal, as all pilgrims do, even now.

During the night Murugan appeared before him and made a divine behest that the Chettiyar should build a proper temple for Him at Verugal. The Chettiyar was overjoyed at this divine manifestation; he soon became aware, where a hidden treasure could be discovered by him, with the proceeds of which, a temple for Muruga Vel was erected at Verugal. On hearing about this, through the Chettiyar, the King of Kandy made endowments to the temple and enriched the Chettiyar also. Quoting 'Lee', S. Kanapathipillai, in his article says that the temple was seen in its glory when visited by him (Lee) having in its possession rich jewels and ornaments, with several Moorthies installed in it and about 1,500 persons serving it. But like all Hindu temples, Verugalampathy also suffered in the hands of the foreigners in the 16th century.

The important event in the temple now is the annual festival which is held for eighteen days during August-September. Pilgrims who go on foot, along the coastal route to Kathirkamam, time their journey to be present at this place for the festival.

As reported in the 'Taprobane' of 1887, by Hugh Neville, a Tamil inscripton has been found in the temple. It records, 'Salutations to Sri Subramaniya. The wall on the south is the gift of Kailaya Vanniyar, the western side the gift of Simmapillai, son of Tamasamakan, the northern side (the gift) of the Karaiyar of Maddakalappur and the

Karaiyar of Negombo, and the gift of Chetties (the eastern side)'.

Reference:

1. Akilesapillai V, 'Thiru Konasala Vaipavam', (Tamil), 1889

2. Kanapathipillai S, 'Chitra Velautha alayam ', an article in 'Thiru Konesar aliya Kumba abisheka malar', (Tamil), 1963

3. Navaratnam C. S, 'A Short History of Hinduism'

60. SIVASUBRAMANIYA SWAMY KOVIL, SLAVE ISLAND, COLOMBO

I became a devotee of this temple in 1949, when I accompanied M. S. Thiruvilangam who was a Managing Trustee; he used to hold bajanai recitals in the temple. Upon his demise, I was entrusted with his place in the management in 1954 but soon gave it up as I was not equal to the task, then. However, I shouldered this sacred task, later in 1962, when the Divine Grace enabled me to set in motion the renovation of the temple and the building of the parivaraha moorthy shrines, which good work has been completed now.

The Siva Subramaniya Swamy Kovil at Kew Road, Slave Island, is one of the oldest Hindu places of worship in the City of Colombo.

The temple structure that we had up to 1962 was the building erected in 1902 by Sir Ponnambalam Ramanathan. The temple that existed at this site before was a smaller structure. The small Subramaniya statue - about six inches in height, now housed at the portals of the Moolasthanam, was then the main deity and the temple was known as Kadiresan Kovil, Slave Island. How this Kadiresan Kovil came to be built is itself of great interest.

As far back as 1822, this Subramaniya Statue was housed, we find from records, in a shrine built by one Periyathamby (and others) in his land at Dam Street, Colombo. The priest who officiated was Sri Ranajee Maha Raajee assisted by one Manickam Pandaram who also held religious classes for the children. Most of the devotees who congregated at the temple for worship were travellers and the shrine was then known as a Pilgrim's Temple. It was a place of worship for the many Service Officers and men who travelled through Colombo from India to Africa, for combat in the Boer War.

In about 1867, Arunasalam Ponnambalam Modliar of the Governor's Gate (father of Sir P. Ramanathan) and Trustee of several Hindu temples was entrusted by Government with the task of erecting a proper temple for housing the Subramaniya deity, as the Dam Street site was required for Government purposes. A sum of £500 was also made available by Government. Under these circumstances, the first temple was erected at Kew Road, Slave Island, in 1870 by Arunasalam Ponnambalam Modliar and dedicated as Kadiresan Kovil, Slave Island, to be remodelled, enlarged and reconstructed by Sir Ponnambalam Ramanathan later in 1902 with the name of Sri Sivasubramaniya Swami Kovil, Slave Island.

This temple (along with the Sivan Temple at Kochchidade) was then looked after by R. Rajendra. In 1942, it was declared a Trust and the Board of Trustees consisting of Messrs. Athiyar, M. C Conniah, Ramasamy Reddiyar, K. T. Vallipuram and C. K. Ratnam were in charge of the affairs of the temple; later, M. S. Thiruvilangam took the President's place on the Board.

Sura Sankaram: Skanda's lance seeks the Asura at Sivasubramaniya Swami Temple, Slave Island

A magnificent reception hall seen at the entrance was erected then along with the excellent Vasantha Mandapam structure.

As the cabook temple structure of over 50 years old was showing signs of decay, proposals were taken in hand in 1962 to renovate and rebuild it, providing also parivara moorthy shrines for Vinayakar, Nadaraja, Maha Vishnu, Saniyasuvarar and Navakgrakam. All these have now been completed and the Kumba Abishekam was elaborately held in 1975. The temple is now a grand structure due to the untiring efforts of the Trustees, only the Raja Gopuram has yet to be erected.

The temple is the haven of solace for thousands of devotees of Muruga Moorthy (Kataragama Deiyo) and all Hindu relgious festivals and pujas are carefully carried out daily, in accordance with the Saivaite Agamas, conventions and rituals. The observance of the Kanthsashdi in October is a special occasion at the temple, when after the Sashdi five day observances, a further five day alankara festival is held culminating with a Vel car procession around Slave Island on the last day.

61. MANDUR KANDASWAMY TEMPLE, BATTICALOA

Referred to by devotees as Thillai Mandur Thiru Sthalam, this Murugan temple is situated by the Batticaloa Lake, about twenty miles in the interior, south of Batticaloa.

The legend concerning the origin of this Veddah shrine of yore is similar to that of other Muruga places of worship, in the eastern coastal region. One of the three splintering rays which emanated, when Vahura hill was split open, by God Skanda, was sheltered among the Thillai trees of Mandur. The Veddah clan who occupied these areas, reverently treasured it and it became their place of worship, with some sort of a simple shrine built there of poles, sticks, and leaves. Later, the simple shrine assumed the shape of a temple when it was patronised by the folks who took up permanent abode there, being engaged in cultivation and fishing.

Like other Hindu temples of the region, this holy place also was built as a proper Kandaswamy temple during the reign of King Magha (1215-1255). It is recorded that the structure was erected by one of his chieftans named Mandur Nagan, who lived in the mansion Mandur Salai. He is said to have built the Chitra Velautha Swamy temple at Porai, also, which is in the vicinity.

The management today carefully observes simple Veddah rituals in the day-to-day ceremonies of the temple which are very much similar to those observed at the shrine at Kadirkamam. The Moolasthana Moorthy in the sanctum is not exposed to view and pujas are performed behind a curtain.

The location of the site of the temple, by the Batticaloa Lake, lends itself to a picturesque setting. Large shady trees pervade the praharas and the temple faces south where the Lake waters lap. The setting is ideal for complete relaxation and no wonder several devotees have been inspired to write poetic compositions about Mandur.

The annual festival, lasting for twenty days, concludes with the theertham on the full moon day in the month of August. During the festival, as at Kadirkamam, the deity is taken to the Valli shrine and back, but remains there for the rest of the day after theertham.

A special feature is the Kantha Shasti observance in October. The Thiruchendur Puranam is read, and at the end, the divine nuptials of Murugan to the Veddah Princess Valli Ammai are celebrated with much ado, when all present take part in the ceremony.

Kavadi Aaddam is a particular feature of the Mandur festivals, when troupe after troupe are seen engaged in most intricate dance forms.

The story is narrated locally, how a Portuguese party who arrived there to demolish the temple were unable to withstand the sting of wasps, and had to flee leaving behind their swords, spears and guns, which remain there today.

I came to be within His orbit when engaged on the Gal-Oya Scheme and the construction of the Mandur Distributory Irrigation Channel; I am indebted to Vidwan Pandit V. S. Kandiah for information concerning this sylvian shrine.

Reference:

There are several compositions about Mandur Thiru Sthalam. Some of which are: The Mandur Pathikam, The Mandur Iraddai Malai, Mandur Kavady Virutham and the Mandur Murugamalai.

62. UKANTHA MALAI VELAUTHA SWAMY TEMPLE, OKANDA, BATTICALOA

At the foothills of Okanda Malai is the Ukantha Malai Velautha Swamy or Kandaswamy Temple, dedicated to God Skanda. His shrines are often found on hilltops.

The site has been referred by tradition as one of the places where Emperor Ravana halted for worship etc, on his journeys from Lanka Puram to Koneswaram.

Okanda hill top has by long tradition been cited as one of the places where a divine ray (kadir), from Lord Skanda struck.

The story may be read on the next page, in this compilation. As at that site, the Veddahs preserved the sanctity of the place with a simple shrine of sticks and Ola leaves.

On the top of the hill we find today a 'well' structure which has been preserved. It is said that this is one of the eight separate wells sunk in different directons, during the regime of the Vanniyas, who came to Lanka along with Kulakoddan of Konesar Temple fame. His son Singa Kumaran is said to have had a temple erected on the hill top and sunk these eight wells.

In the small temple found today regular worship and pujas are held. The annual festivals are held for fifteen days concluding with the new moon day in July.

63. CHITRA VELAUTHA KANDASWAMY KOVIL, THIRUKOVIL, BATTICALOA

Along the eastern coast, about 50 miles south of Batticaloa, is the settlement of Thirukovil, which gains its name from its central feature, viz: an ancient Hindu temple. The carefully preserved vimanam which remains today, over the sanctum, though oversize, with its pillars, half pillars and decorative motifs, has helped archaeologists to identify this temple as of Pandyan architecture of the 13th century.

Thirukovil: The temple with a precious Vimanam of old

Legends associate this site as being one of the stopping places of Emperor Ravana, of the Ramayana era, on his way to Trincomalee to worship at Koneswaram. Ravana, who is said to have been a devout worshipper of Lord Siva, always carried with him the golden emblem of Siva - the Siva Lingam, to which he would perform abishekam and puja ceremonies wherever he stops in his journey.

Invariably a Sivan Temple would get founded at such places and Thirukovil is said to be one such Sacred (Thiru) Temple (Kovil).

Leaving the era of myths and traditions, we learn that in the early historical period, the eastern coastal belt of Lanka was occupied by Veddahs. Veddahs are hunters. They survived by the use of the spear and the bow and arrow. To them these were fundamental to their existence and to their command over the animal kingdom. So legends are woven around these and it is not surprising that the spear or the lance, which became to be represented by a 'Vel', became a symbol or emblem of worship. We come across such instances of origin of worship, in many of Batticaloa's sacred places of today. It has been so at Verugal Kandaswamy Temple, Mandur Kandaswamy Temple and the Okanda Temple. The same is true of the temple at Thirukovil.

The Batticaloa Manmiam narrates an interesting legend. When God Skanda defeated the Asuras, he was confronted by the Vahura hill, which He split into two. Three splintering rays which originated thence from the ocean, were sheltered, one on the Okanda Hill top, one on a white naval tree at Thirukovil and the third on a thillai tree at Mandur. Subsequently all these places were reverentially observed as holy places by the Veddahs. Worship commenced at these, with simple shrines put up with sticks and poles and Ola leaves.

It is said that during the days of Walugam Bhava (103 B. C.) the seven Chola Chiefs who led a second Tamil invasion had this simple primitive shrine constructed as a proper structure, erecting it facing east instead of the northern facing adopted by the Veddahs.

The location was some kind of a port in the ancient days, and was known as Nagar Munai Thurai. As to how a proper statutory agamic Hindu temple came to be built there and how it earned its name of Thirukovil, we read in the 'Manmiam.' It is said that at the time when one Prasanna Sithu was the local chief, there came a Kalinga Prince by the name of Bhuvaneha Gaja Bahu who was travelling on pilgrimage to Rameswaram, Koneswaram and Thirukethiswaram with his family. The local chief received them. They were highly pleased at the reception given to them that the Princess, who was a Chola, expressed a desire to build a grand temple here. This was soon accomplished with the aid of sthapathy-artists and craftsmen from her home (Chola) country. This was the first grand temple erected at the site and perhaps in the whole region, and so it was given (and earned) the name of the Thiru (Sacred) Kovil (Temple). Today, not only the temple, but even the settlement is known as Thirukovil.

The Princess's name Thampathy Nallal became perpetuated by the vicinity earning the name Thampathy Villu or Thambiluvil of today. They decided to settle down here and were given the neighbouring Southern area which they developed with great success. That was in the era of the year 28 AC. Their son Prince Manu Neya Gaja Bahu continued the work that his father had founded in their Southern Unarisi kingdom and discharged his life-long desire of improving the Thirukovil temple into even a grander structure with a seven tiered sthoopi and several additonal works. That was said to be during the years 48 AC and after, when there was also constructed Sagamam Kulam, at the foot hills of Sangamam Kandi, for irrigated cultivation needs.

We gather glimpses about the temple that was at the site, later, in the Pandyan Era. Authentic evidence of this is gained from a Tamil inscription discovered by Hugh Neville. Writing in the 'Taprobanian' (Vol.1, p. 84) he says 'I propose to edit from time to time in this Journal such Tamil inscriptions as may be discovered in Ceylon. I now give one conveying land to the Sivagnana Sankarar Kovil, now known as Thirukovil in the Batticaloa District'. The inscription records the gift of a tract of paddy fields named Vovila (extent about 350 acres) on the 20th day of the month of 'Thai' by Sri Vijayabahu Devar alias Sri Sangabodhipramar, Emperor of the three worlds, in his tenth regnal year, to Sivagnana Sangarar Kovil. It further stipulates that anyone who destroys this charity will accumulate the sin of killing the Karam pasu (tawny cows) on the banks of the River Ganges. The name of the king has been identified as either Vijayabahu III 1240-1267 AC) or Vijayabahu VI (1398-1410 AC).

Another inscription discovered in 1967, at the temple, has been deciphered by A. Veluppillai, and refers to the gift of some land or building (indistinct) to the temple which is referred to as Chitra Velautha Swamy Kovil. This inscription is said to have been of the sixteenth century.

The temple, like most other Hindu shrines, was destroyed by the Portuguese. Paul E. Pieris writes in 'Ceylon and Portuguese Era' - Part 1, p. 323, that even the settlement was abandoned by its inhabitants upon the destruction of the temple and the murder of the temple staff.

Rev. Queroz a historian and Portuguese priest, describes the temple structure as having had three Gopurams at the time of destruction.

It is found that sometime in the later Dutch or early British period, when there was a general resuscitation of Hinduism in the Island, merchantmen, who were trading with India erected at the site a temple, dedicating it to Skanda, Kadirai-Andavan, at this Kandapananturai, or the port of Kandan's arrow. Chief Justice Alexander Johnston writes, in 1806, in the R. A. S. Journal, Vol XXXVI - No. 98, p. 74, that he went to Thirukovil, on his circuit to the Batticaloa District. He had conversed with the young Tanjore Brahmin priest in charge. The temple now faced the sea (East) but formerly it had faced the land (?). Reference is made to the temple ratham constructed about three years earlier and to the temple devadasies and other servants of the temple.

We thus get glimpses of Thirukovil's ancient past: - mythology attributes sanctity to the place where Emperor Ravanan did his Siva-pujas, the Veddahs treasured the site, as a resting place of a ray (Kadir) from God Skanda, early historical era saw two splendid traditional temples, of Chola architecture - those would have been the days of glory at Thirukovil! After centuries, a temple with the name of Sivagnana Sangarar Kovil is known to have existed therein about the 14th century, which was the structure the Portuguese demolished. A temple has subsequently been erected which is there now.

Little did I realise, when I used to frequent the place during the years 1950-55, in connection with Gal Oya Right Bank Irrigation Scheme and effecting improvement to Sagamam tank, that this temple with its peculiar appearance, with a precious Vimanam (though oversize on the present structure), had such revered antiquity.

Today pujas and other rituals are performed here regularly. The annual festivals are held for ten days, terminating with the new moon day in July-August, besides which a special event is the festival in April. The place is one of the landmarks on the eastern coast where pilgrims who go on foot along the coastal route to Kadirkamam, halt and rest for a time.

64. KATARAGAMA DEVIYO, SKANDA SHRINE, KADIRKAMAM

Thousands flock to Kadirkamam for worship. To the Buddhists the deity of this sacred site is Kataragama Deviyo and to the Hindus He is Skanda or Murugan.

Skanda Purana, a puranic legend in Sanskrit, narrates the story of Skanda emanating as six sparks to be fondled by the Kartikeya Maidens in Lake Saravana and becoming one child of exquisite beauty, when clasped by Uma. Defeating the Titan Asuran, with his lance 'Vel', Skanda released the Devas from torture and was given Devai Yanai, Indra's daughter in marriage. Further, according to legends he falls in love with Valliamma, a Vedda girl and takes abode at the hill top of Kataragama. Subsequently, years later, Kalyan giri, a sage from India, who became to be known as Muthu Linga Swamy, unable to persuade Him to return, also continued to dwell at Kataragama. His, it is said, is the sacred Yantra or tablet, the chief object of worship today at Kataragama. This has been the place of pilgrimage of Sinhalese Kings from pre-Christian days. The Bo-tree is associated with Devanampia Tissa and the Kiri Vihara with King Dutugemunu; these and others came to Kataragama, beseeching favours. The main shrine is a simple structure; there are other temples.

The Maha-Devale is the foremost place of worship, as it holds within it the Yantra, the holy object; its nature is a secret, known only to the chief kapurales. Wirz thinks that it may be a gold leaf with a hexagonal (formed by two triangles placed on top of each other) emblem of Skanda, engraved on it. The small box containing it is taken out, with all reverence, during Perahera processions. Adjoining the Maha-Devale are the Vishnu and the Ganesha devales. The Valli Amme devale is further away. In the vicinity are also the Theiva Yanai and the Bhairaver temples. The Muthulinga Swamy shrine is near the Valli Amme Devala. Other places of Hindu worship are the Pillaiyar Temple at Sella-Kadirkamam and the shrine at Kadiramalai hill-top.

The Esala-Perahera, the main festival at Kataragama, is held for fifteen days ending with the water-cutting ceremony on full-moon day, in July-August. It is a grand occasion when thousands of pilgrims gather and religious fervour is at its highest ever. The other two festivals are the Illmaka Kachi Perahera in November-December and the Aluth Avuruthu Perahera on NewYears day, in April.

Publications:

There are several publications in Tamil, on Kadirkamam. Among those in English are:

Arunachalam, Sir Ponnambalam 'The worship of Muruga or Skanda' - R.A.S. 1925
Wirz, Ven Paul, 'Kataragama' Lake House, Publishers 1966

65. EARLY TEMPLES OF NALLUR, JAFFNA.

Nallur was the celebrated capital city of ancient Jaffna. After Kathiramalai (Kantherodai), Singai Nagar and Nallur flourished as the capital of the Jaffna Kingdom. The chronicle of Jaffna history, the Yalpana Vaipava Malai (ref 1) describes in detail how the city of Nallur was founded. It mentions how Singai Ariyan arrives at the request of Pandi Maluvan accompanied by priests and advisers and assumes the kingship of Jaffna. He builds a city for his residence and names it Nallur. Description is made of the place that was built with lofty walls and towers, hall of justice, army camps, stables for elephants and horses etc; the celebrated Yamuneri Theertham, was excavated amidst them all and made holy with sacred waters from the Yamuna river close to the Himalyas.

Thus was founded the celebrated city of Nallur by Singai Ariyan, also referred to as Kulankai, who commenced his reign as the First Ariya Chakravarty King of Jaffna. Several reasons are given for the selection of this location (ref 2): it having been a military outpost of the Pandyan Armies who were in the North in the 13th century, it being the residence of Maluvan who invited Singai Ariyan to assume charge of the Kingdom. It was given the name of Nallur which was a significant place in Singai Ariyan's homeland.

It is now believed that it continued to be the capital city of the Singai Ariyan Kings of Jaffna, with the appropriate name of the city (nagar) of the Singai Royalty or Singai Nagar. That Singai Nagar was Vallipuram as believed once has now been discountenanced.

There are two schools of thought regarding the time or the era when Singai Ariyan arrived to assume the kingdom. Rasanayaga Mudaliyar, basing his inferences on the Jaffna Chronicles, had deduced Kulanka's reign as having been from 1210 AC to 1256 AC when Kulasekera Singai succeeded him. Based on other evidence, eminent present day historians have suggested a later date, viz. 1284 AC, as being the more probable year of commencement of the Ariya Chakravarty rule in Jaffna.

The Temples around the city of Nallur

Divine protection to the celebrated city was sought by building the Saddanathar Kovil at its northern approach. Saddanathar, in Hindu mythology, represents a forceful personality of the Supreme Parameswaran.

To the east of the city was erected the Veiyul Ukantha Pillaiyar Kovil.

The Kailaya Pillaiyar temple was erected in the southern approaches to the city.

The Veera Maha Kali Amman Kovil was founded at the western approaches of the city. It was the scene of a battle during the reign of King Sangili.

Two more temples, viz. Thaiyal Nayaki Ammal Kovil and Salai Vinayakar Kovil, are listed (ref 3) which have not been identified.

These six were the first of the temples erected during Singai Ariyan's regime.

The Singai Ariya dynasty continued to rule as Ariya Chakravarty Kings of Jaffna, assuming alternately the state titles of Pararajasekaram and Segarajasekaram. They safeguarded the Hindu temples by building more in the kingdom and maintaining those already erected. They upheld the Hindu religion. The Kailaiya Natha temple described earlier, was one of the special temples which the king erected. As described by a historian (ref 4) 'The king who had long cherished in his mind the idea of building at Nallur a temple for Siva, whom he had worshiped at Madurai in the form of Cokkanatan, started to construct it at an auspicious time'; 'a magnificent temple of large dimensions, presumably it was one of the largest of religious monuments within the kingdom' describes the temple well.

Kandaswamy temple of the Tamil Kings

The Jaffna Chronicle also records that (ref 5) during the reign of Singai Ariyan, Minister Bhuvaneka Bahu completed the erection of the outside walls of the city and Kandaswamy Kovil. That a Kandaswamy temple gets erected within the city of Nallur, during the reign of Singai Ariyan thus becomes explicitly recorded and the credit for this 'Thiruppany' work goes to the King's Minister, Bhuvenaka Bahu. The time would have been soon after the year 1284 AC. Unlike in the case of the Kailaya Natha temple, not much is said about the structure itself. It has to be therefore presumed to have been of humbler proportions.

Of interest is the traditional Kaddiyam, recited devotedly on all festive occasions, at the present Kandaswamy temple at Nallur. Reference is made to 'Sri Maharajathi Raja... Srimat Sanghabodhi Bhuvaneka Bahu ...' The exalted personage referred to is very likely to be Sapumal, who was sent by the King of Kotte to subdue the Jaffna kingdom in the year 1450. He took possession of the kingdom and ruled over Jaffna from 1450 AC to 1467, eventually assuming the title of Sangabodhi Bhuvenaka Bahu. It is said that towards the end of his reign he effected improvements to the town of Singai Nagar, renovating and erecting new buildings, maybe to endear himself with the people. It may also be inferred that he would have built up the Kandaswamy temple to proper traditional requirements and thereby earn his name in the kaddiyam tradition. That would have been probably sometime during the year 1460 to 1467 AC.

As to what this temple was like or what became, of it, we read in subsequent history. Father Queroz, the Portuguese priest and historian, who accompanied their invading forces, records (ref 6) that the large pagoda at Nallur was demolished to ground level in the year 1621. Subsequently the Dutch, who found a Catholic Church there, demolished it and erected a church of their faith, which may be the Nallur Church that is seen today, in close proximity to the Yamuneri Theertham.

Entrance to the Royal Palace of the Jaffna Kings
Remnants of Archway seen at Nallur today

Today such place names as Pandarakulam, Pandara malikai, Sangilithoppu remain to remind us of this Royal region. More tangible remnants are the ruins seen today at Nallur of the stone masonry arched gate way, seen in the picture. Opposite to this, across the roadway is an old bungalow called 'manthiri manai', residence of a minister, even now in use. These are said to have been repaired and put into use during the days of the Dutch occupation. Some ornamental statue work may yet be seen in them.

'Manthiri Manai'
The Residence of a Minister during the era of the Jaffna Kingdom
seen opposite the archway at Nallur, today.

Worship of Kumara Vel or Skanda Kumaran in Ancient Lanka

Worship of Kumara Vel or Skanda Kumaran seems to have been prevalent in Ancient Lanka; the northern regions which had come into contact later with Chola culture in the 9th and 10th centuries would have had temples for worship of Kumaran or the Kandaswamy deity. As at Maviddapuram or Kandavanakadavai, there would have been in Nallur, an important outpost, places of worship for Muruga Vel which later would have become some sort of shrine, which distinguished personages, as Minister Bhuvaneka Vahu or King Bhuveneka Bahu, would take every step to reconstruct and enlarge as a traditional agamic temple.

Reverence to Muruga Vel seems to have been prevalent even during the pre- historic era. Discovery of urn burials, similar to those found in South India, containing emblems of Vel, are being discovered in coastal locations in Sri Lanka too. Megalithic burial layer was discovered recently, on the 29th November 1980 at Anaikoddai, only 2 or 3 miles from Nallur. Partially damaged urn and a metal biscriptual seal make it of special interest. Subsequently others are being discovered in the Peninsula. It is quite possible that the origin of Nallur temples may have been in the ancient eras.

The Present Kandaswamy Temple

The present Nallur Kandaswamy temple was originated in the year 1749 by Ragunatha Mappana Mudaliyar. A description of this most venerated temple of today, its pujas and festivals appears elsewhere in this book.

References:

1.   'Yalpana Vaipava Malai' edited by Kula Sabanathan, 1953, pp 25 - 26

2 & 3. Pathmanathan, S. 'The kingdom of Jaffna' 1978, p. 187, 194

4 & 5. 'Yalpana Vaipava Malai', p. 26, p. 31

6.   'Spiritual conquest of Ceylon', Fr. Queroz, p. 642

66. KANTHAVANA KADAVAI TEMPLE POLIHANDY, VALVETTITURAI

This fascinating shrine had enchanted me from my very early days. I can well recollect my being taken there when I was young sometime about the year 1917, for the performance of a vow to Arumuga swamy. It was just a small simple structure, extended for the festival period with several cadjan pandals. The fast growing creeper of the Valli Yam, ceremoniously planted each year, received the veneration of all Murugan's devotees. Symbolically, it depicted maid Valli Ammai's welcome to youthful Skanda Kumaran.

Whatever that may have been, we now have a well built Sri Kandaswamy temple at the historic site in Polihandy near Valvetiturai along the north coast road of the Jaffna Peninsula.

The origin of this sthalam is the legend that one day a Vigrakam statue of the Kandaswamy Murthi was cast ashore from the ocean, on the Valvetithurai beach. It was devoutly collected by the local folks and enshrined. This may have taken place during the period of the Chola occupation of the country, which was an era of Hindu religious significance. So the location became Kanda Vanam and the term Kadavai means 'crossed over'. All this is tradition and no supporting evidence is available. Whatever that may be, Kandavanam became a revered place. Any temple or shrine there may have been, would have been devastated along with others in the 16th century.

Historically we have the interesting story of how the Arumuga swamy moorthi vigrakam became to be available for dharisanam to Muruga devotees at this location. A group of merchants from the Jaffna Peninsula had proceeded to the hinterland for trade. Enroute they had come across an exquisitely carved Sanmuga Vigrakam lying abandoned in the jungles of Kumarapuram in the Vanni, off Mullaitivu. In keeping with their vow, on the satisfactory completion of their mission they had brought the Vigrakam to this sthalam for worship.

Very soon a temple was built by the forefathers of the present management and Kandavanam became an important Muruga sthalam, with the unique feature of having a Sanmuga vigrakam in the sanctum. At the temple today we have the utsava Murthi which is also an Arumuga Swamy vigrakam. A Muthu Cumaraswamy shrine and a parivaraha Vinayaka shrine adorn the temple.

The ancient Arumuga Swamy Vigrakam now presides in a shrine in the northern prahara for tharisanam by all devotees. It has the unique feature of the entire complement of Arumuga Swamy with the two consorts Deivayanai and Valli mounted on a peacock, seen standing on one foot, carved from a single stone.

67. KANDASWAMY MALAI RUINS, KOKKILAI LAGOON, MULLAITIVU

Along the North Eastern Coastal region of the Island, in the Kokkilai Lagoon, about two miles from Thennai maravadi, were found the ruins of a Hindu place of worship. These were discovered during Archaeological Investigations during 1905 and the findings have been reported in the Archaeological Commissioner's Report (ref 1).

Located at Kandasami Malai, 96 feet in elevation, in the current topographic maps, it is situated right on the tip of a promontory jutting out into the lagoon, with water almost around it. It is reached from Tennamaraivadi, an important settlement at the outfall of Mora Oya across which the Padawiya Reservoir has been constructed. It is about 25 miles south, along the coast from Mullaitivu.

The ruins, it is reported, are of a small Sivan Temple, built of stones of exquisite workmanship comparable to those of the Chola Siva Devales found at Polonnaruwa (ref 2).

References:

1. Archaeological Commissioner's Annual Report for 1905

2. Indrapala, Dr. K., 'Dravidian Architecture in Ceylon'. 1970, p. 29

68. SITHANDI KANDASWAMY KOVIL, BATTICALOA

A Muruga temple where large numbers of devotees gather for worship is the Kandaswamy Kovil, known as Chitravelautha Swamy Kovil, situated by the main road at Sithandi, 12 miles north of Batticaloa. It is verily Batticaloa's equivalent of the Nallur Kandaswamy temple at Jaffna.

Like many of the Muruga sthalams in the eastern region, tradition has it that this Kumara Vel sannithanam too originated from the era of Veddah antiquity. It is said that once upon a time an 'Andy', a saintly personage, was traversing this area, then in jungle, to Kataragama on pilgrimage. When affronted by a rogue elephant about to charge, he took from his pouch a betel leaf and shaping it like a Vel, invoked Kumara Vel's aid by chanting the Sadaksha mantiram, upon which the elephant went away subdued and the party enjoyed safe journey. In due course the venerable person, settled down here, and around his shrine for Kumara Vel, there grew a Veddah hamlet. Many miracles were attributed to Andi's shrine and he himself became known as Sith-Andi (the miraculous mendicant) munivar or Sikandi Munivar.

Upon his demise the location became even more venerable and very soon the settlement developed into a well established village of well-to-do devotees. The humble shrine was also built up into a proper temple complete with all agamic requirements of a Kandaswamy temple. Today the majestic temple tower is imposing and spacious mandapams and alluring prahara murthi shrines adorn this sannithanam. Thousands of devotees flock there for Murukan's Grace and be inspired by Sithandi Munivars holy vibrations.

The annual mahotsava festival held in August is an occasion when large numbers of devotees gather and several festive features are arranged. The last three days, in particular, are very special because of the 'Maiyal Kadduth' festival.

References:-

There are many publications about Sithandi temple.

1.   Sithandi Thiru Sthala Puranam by A. N. Allakesa Mudaliyar

2.   A booklet of 'Unjal' songs by S. Kathiramalai (1954)

3.   More than one poet has offered garlands of verses

4.   A 'Temple Puranam' of 200 stanzas, exlolling the Sthalam has been published recently.

5.   'Maddak Kalappu Makkal Vallamum Valkaiyam' (Tamil) compiled by F.X.C. Nadarasa (1980).

69. CHITRA VELAUTHA SWAMY KOVIL, PORATIVU, BATTICALOA

Fifteen miles south of Batticaloa is the celebrated Eruvil Porativu eastern coastal region of Sri Lanka. Eruvil or Erakavil gets referred to in the early annals of Lanka. History has recorded the existence of a Hindu temple in Erakavila, early in the third century, which was important enough to have incurred the displeasure of Lanka's reigning monarch. It was one of the Brahminical temples destroyed in the third century, records the Maha Vamsa (ref 1).

Local tradition (ref 2) has it that the region was once a well developed kingdom of Mandu Nagan who reigned in Nagan cholai, near Mandur. He had Nagar chieftains and Yakkar ministers. There were temples for the Hindu deities and stately palaces. All of which got destroyed and the region become to be named Kali-thesam.

Kanapathipilai writes (ref 2) that when King Mahinda was ruling over Lanka, the eastern region was looked after by a local chieftan named Mathi Suthan (1107-1118) (ref 3) dwelling in Kali-thesam. Among the measures taken by him to rebuild Kali-thesam was to re-erect the temple for Sri Murukan, called the Chitra Velautha Swamy Kovil at Porativu. It is said that sculptors and artists were recruited from Thondai Nadu in S. India and a majestic structure erected for the worship of Chitra maura Sankara Vel. It was completed with a five tiered sthoopi, Kopuravasal and necessary mandapams. Regular annual utsava festivals were instituted. He also re-erected the Kandasamy temple at Mandur.

In the course of centuries, due to neglect and devastation the above temple went into ruins and decay. However the incumbent Velautha Swamy deity has been installed in the present Chitra Velautha Swamy Kovil erected by Nagappa Chettiyar at Kovil Porativu about two miles west of Kaluvanchikudi. It is now under the able management of leading residents and regular annual utsava festivals are held in the month of August

Lands and paddy fields were said to have been bequeathed for the maintenance of the temple by King Magha in the thirteenth century.

References:

1.   Mahavamsa XXXVII 42

2.   Kanapathipillai S., 'Poorvika Saptha Sthalankal,' Tamil, 1979, pp 23 - 26

3.   Kandiah V. S., 'Madda Kalappu Tamilakam, 1964, p. 436

SECTION IV

VISHNU TEMPLES

70. VENERATION OF MAHA VISHNU

Maha Vishnu is venerated by large number of devotees as the Preserver of the Universe. Lord Vishnu is one of the Thirumurthi Gods of the Hindu Pantheon. In Sri Lanka he is specially revered as the custodian of the Island. Vaishnavites venerate him as the Supreme Deity. The Vishnu Purana, a work of the 1st century B.C. extols his attributes.

Known in early Vedic times as a manifestation of solar energy, he later becomes a deity of major importance and along with Brahma and Siva formed the holy Thirumuthikal of Hinduism. All things emanate from him say the Vaishnavites. In mythology, while Brahma performs creation, Vishnu preserves the lives of all and sundry in the universe. He is the embodiment of goodness and mercy. Because of his acts of Preservation and Duration, he is a symbol of perpetual life and earns the name 'Narayana' meaning 'the abode of man'

Aum Namo Narayana
Aum Namo Narayana!

His Representation

Like all Hindu representations, the image of Vishnu also manifests his attributes. Usually he is seen in a standing pose. The four arms are indicative of power in all the four directions. The lower right arm has a mace, the upper a lotus; the left upper arm has conch and the lower a discus. The mace represents knowledge and the lotus the universe. The conch is symbolic of the five elements, and when blown gives out the primodial note. The revolving discus, shining like the sun, represents the mind and with its spikes has unlimited power to destroy. Maha Vishnu is always depicted in dark-blue, which is the colour of the ether or space pervading the universe.

In the temples, in addition to the standing pose installed in the sanctum, Vishnu Murthi is also seen in a reclining pose as Ananda Sayana Perumal. He is reclining in slumbers on 'Sesa' the coiled serpant, floating on water. Sesa is sometimes named as 'Ananda' and his coils reprent endless time.

His Consort

Lord Vishnu's consort is Maha Lakshmi. According to mythology she arose from the milky ocean when it was churned by the Devas in search of the elixir of perpetual life. She became the Divine Consort of Maha Vishnu, who was master-minding the churning operation. She is personified as the embodiment of grace and charm and is venerated as the Goddess of well being and fortune. She is usually depicted standing or seated on a lotus pedestal. It is customary to find a picture or figure of the goddess at the entrance of every Hindu home as an assurance of well-being.

His Vahana or Steed

Lord Vishnu's steed is the mythical bird 'Garuda' it has the face and beak of a vulture and the body of a human. It is conceived as very powerful and strong enough to convey Vishnu in all his journeys to the cosmic and nether worlds. It is a serpent devouring bird and the Garuda mantra is an antidote against snake poisoning.

At all Vishnu temples the statue of Garuda occupies a prominant place in the front, facing the deity. During festivals the Garuda vahana is frequently used to convey the deity.

The Avatars or Incarnations

As Preserver and Protector of all life in the universe, it is incumbent on Maha Vishnu to keep the entire world functioning along the lines of righteousness. He therefore assumes birth known as appearences or 'Avatars' in various Forms to re-establish when wrong prevails, as the Bhaved Gita declares:

Whenever there is decay of righteousness
and rise of un-righteousness
Then I myself shall come forth.
To destroy the unrighteous,
To save the Righteous,
and to establish righteousness.
I come into Being, from age to age.

There are ten major Avatars of Vishnu cited in the Puranas.

1. The Matsya Avatar or the fish incarnation: Once when a great deluge destroyed the whole world, he as a fish, rescued Manu to originate the present human race.

2. The Kurma Avatar or the tortoise incarnation: As a tortoise he descends to the bottom of the ocean to assist in the recovery of the life giving Elixir of life and save the Devas from extinction.

3. The Varaha Avatar or the boar incarnation: As a boar he saved the world when it was drowned in the ocean by a demon.

4. Narasimha Avatar: Incarnating as a man-lion he destroyed Iranian who was ill treating a Vishnu devotee.

5. Vamana Avatar: Incarnating as a dwarf he won back for the Devas their dominion.

6. Parasurama Avatar, as the great Parasurama he restored the power of the priests.

7. Ramachandra; as the able Rama Bahavan he destroys the wicked and restores righteousness.

8.   The Bala Rama Avatar is another mythical hero who fought for and established righteousness.

9.   Gautama Buddha founds Buddhism giving value to righteousness.

10.   The Kalki Avatar is yet to happen.

Temples

There are several temples in Sri Lanka for the worship of Maha Vishnu. Some of these are described in the pages that follow; as he has been revered from very ancient times, ruins of ancient Vishnu temples and several ancient statues of the deity, have been unearthed at various places in the island.

71. VARATHARAJA VENKADESA PERUMAL KOVIL, JAFFNA TOWN

This Vishnu temple is situated in the heart of Jaffna Town. Its origin is well known to history. Among the Ariya Chakravarti Kings who ruled the Kingdom of Jaffna, for three centuries from the thirteenth to the sixteenth, there was Kuna Pooshana Singai Ariyan who reigned as Ariya Chakravarti King Sega Raja Sekaram. Kuna Pooshanan was a very successful ruler and a pious king. He was very much interested in the development of his little kingdom. For this purpose we read in history, that he invited settlers, especially proficient in finer weaving, from Andra Nad, Karaikal and Kanchipuram in South India. Among them it is said there was a devout religious man who assisted the settlers in their customary Vaishnava form of worship. The practice was originally commenced under a tree and continued thereafter. The tree being only a tree, had survived the devastation done to places of worship during the Portuguese and the Dutch days. Homage is paid even today, to this age old tree, where a figure has been erected in memory, and daily pujas arc performed.

Perumal Kovil, Jaffna,

The temple is well maintained and there are shrines for Sri Rama Chandra, Gopalan, Lakshmi and Andal Devi for all of whom daily pujas are performed.

Recently along with the renovation, architectural features have been added to the temple structure, together with a new seven-tiered Raja Gopuram. In the Gopuram structure is embodied figures featuring traditional events, mentioned in the various avatharams of Krishna, Rama Bhagavan, the Ramayana episode and Gopalan's antics with the Gopies.

The annual festival at the temple takes place in September-October.

72. PONNALAI VARATHARAJA PERUMAL TEMPLE, THOLPURAM, JAFFNA

'The oldest temple in Jaffna, dedicated to Rama and Krishna, were at Vallipuram and Punnalai respectively and they are mentioned in the Kohila Sandesa', writes Mudaliyar C. Rasanayagam.

This Vishnu temple, dedicated to Varatha Raja Perumal, is an ancient temple, situated at Ponnalai, near Tholpuram. Tholpuram itself means the township where traditions prevail. Like all ancient Hindu temples, the origin of Varatharaja Perumal temple at Ponnalai is also legendary. The story is narrated by Soothai Maha Muniver in the twenty second chapter of the Dakshana Kailasa Manmiam, which is a part of the ancient Sanskrit Skanda Purana; in the seas west of Ponnalai, a turtle was found trapped in a fisherman's net. He brought it ashore and as he could not carry it alone, he sought the aid of his people but when they came, the turtle had turned into a stone and there were golden rays shining from the sky above. Attributing this to the advent of Sri Devi (Maha Lakshmi), they decided to build a Vishnu temple here and dedicate it to Varatha Raja Perumal. The turtle stone is there in the sanctum today.

This episode is recorded as Koorma Avatharam of Lord Vishnu. Indiran, King of the Devas, had to be born a fisherman according to a curse by Thurvasa Munivar and would obtain his release when he traps the Lord (in turtle form). He would then ascend to Indra Lokam, in his golden chariot which would await him. Where the Lord's sacred feet trod, became sanctified and to this day it is revered as Thiru Adi Nilayam (Sacred spot of the imprint of the Lord), and the temple which got founded due to the advent of Lakshmi (goddess of wealth) is given the name of Pon (golden) Alayam (temple). The advent of Indiran's golden chariot to this spot on earth, associates it with gold hence the place earned the name of Swarnalaiyam which in Tamil is Ponalayam. Ibn Batuta the celebrated ancient Chinese traveller refers to the worship of the sacred foot at Adams Peak and at this place, in this Island. Whatever evidence there may have been then, has been washed away by the sea.

Legends apart, the area abounds in historical and archaeological interest. In the vicinity was the ancient sea port of Samputhurai or Jambukovalam, which figures in the ancient history of Lanka, where the Romans and Babylonians from the west traded with the Chinese from the east. The Mahawamsa refers to township of Jambukovalam Pattana. It was here that Princess Sangamitta landed with the sacred Bo tree, on her way to Anuradhapura. King Gaja Bahu also landed here bringing with him the tradition of Pattini Kannakai Amman worship to Lanka. References are also made to a Sambeswaram temple in the locality built by King Thissai Maluvan.

In its glorious days of the fifteenth century, according to the Sinhalese poem 'Sandesaya', this temple had seven praharams, with stone masonry walls surrounding it. It was also reputed to have had a golden vimanam (dome) which perpetuated its pristine name of Pon Alayam (The Golden Temple). It then succumbed to the hands of the invaders in the 16th century. It is said that when this edifice was demolished, the stones were removed to Kayts and Manipay tor building work.

Ponalai Varatharaja Perumal Temple
The temple commemorates the Koorma Avatharam of Lord Vishnu,
an episode found in the Vishna Puranam

However, with the resucitation of Hinduism in the ninteenth century, a Vishnu temple was erected at the site; it is dedicated to Varatha Raja Perumal, and is managed and maintained well.

In 1965, when the temple priest Sri La Sri Suppiah Kurukkal, at the ripe age of over seventy years, was relaxing, it is said that the Lord appeared betore him and made a behest for the installation of a 'Reclining Pose' of the Lord, in the temple. Accordingly a magnificent 'Ananda Sayana Perumal' moorthy has since been installed (1971).

The temple is visited daily by many devotees; regular pujas and festivals are keenly observed. Two annual festivals take place in July tor 21 days, and in December for 10 days, terminating with the Swarga Loga Ehathesi.

73. VALLIPURA ALVAR KOVIL, PULOLY, POINT PEDRO

About four miles from Point Pedro on the road to Chempian Pattu is the ancient Vallipuram Temple, dedicated to the worship ot Maha Vishnu. Situated amidst a vast expanse of sand dunes, little reminds us that the area was once a capital city of the Jaffna Kingdom.

The origin of this ancient Vishnu Sthalam is legendary, like all ancient temples. References can be found in the Dakshana Kailasa Puranam and in the Dakshana Kailasa Manmiam under the caption Vallipura Vaipavam. It would appear that the locality was associated from hoary antiquity, with a Vishnavite environment. Thither came Lavalli Ammaiyar, a pious lady. She had been afflicted with a naga-thosham curse and was therefore deprived of having any children. She had been advised to seek this place, sacred to Vishnu, and perform thapas beseeching Him for the remission of her sins. She thus performed thapas daily with arms spread out facing the sea, in the hope that one day Lord Vishnu would appear before her, rising from the ocean (Vishnu Lokam) and grant her the boon.

It was a fishing village, and one day when the fisherfolks cast their nets, an unusually large fish was landed in their boat which started jumping about here and there and finally landed straight into the arms of Lavalli Ammaiyar. As she fondled it, the fish assumed the shape of an infant and to the amazement of everyone had all the appearances of Lord Vishnu himself. The village folks were overjoyed and congratulated themselves on this visitation of the Lord. When the infant vanished an old seer who was present gave to the people a Vishnu Sakkaram, which they decided to install at the spot and venerate it in commemoration of the event. To this day the sakkaram is the chief object of veneration at Vallipuram and is in the sanctum moolasthanam of Vallipuram Alwar Swamy Kovil.

The site has several historical references. A. Mootootamby Pillay in his 'Jaffna History' writes (p. 13) that among those who were brought to settle in Jaffna were some from the North or Thondai Nadu; the place where they settled down assumed the name of Vadamar Achchi (now Vadamarachchi), meaning occupied by the Northerners. That region where Vallia Thevan was the Chief settler, became known as Vallipuram, They were Telugu people and were Vaishnavaites. So a temple for the worship of Sri Vishnu got built at Vallipuram. Mudaliyar Rasanayagam refers to it as the oldest temple in Jaffna, dedicated to Sri Rama Bhagavan.

It was once thought that Singai Nagar, the celebrated City of the Kings of Jaffna, was near Vallipuram. It is now thought that Singai Nagar, the seat of the Singai Ariyan Chakravarti Kings of Jaffna, was Nallur.

Sir Paul E. Pieris made important finds in the vicinity of Vallipuram, as reported by him in the Royal Asiatic Society Journal (Ceylon Branch), Vol. I, No. 3, p. 156. These have been identified as belonging to the period of the first Lambakhana King Vasaba (65-109 AC), and consists of an inscription on gold plate which records 'Hail in the reign of the great king Vasaba and when the Minister Isigiraya was governing Nakadiva, Piyaguka Tissa caused a vihara to be built at Badakara Atana'. It has not been possible, so far to establish the correct identity of the Vihara referred to, with any degree of definiteness.

The Sthoopy

The Sakkaram is the Utsapa Moorthy here

The West Entrance

Vallipuram is one of the oldest temples in Jaffna. In the sanctum is Vishnu's Sakkaram, as mentioned earlier and a venerated Sakkarum occupies the place of the utsava moorthy or the deity that is taken out in processions. In the adjoining shrine, facing south is found Lord Vishnu Himself, entrancingly divine. In the praharam is found the Vinayaka shrine in the usual south-west corner and next to it is a Naga-thambiran shrine; Nachchiar shrine is found at the north-west corner, facing south and Hanuman occupies the shrine where usually Bhairavar is located in Sivan Temples. The navagraham shrine in the usual place completes the prahara shrines.

The temple attracts large crowds of worshippers daily and on Sundays, in particular. A very efficient management which took charge in 1976 deserves the gratitude of every devotee for the systematic arrangement of the functions of this Devasthanam. Pujas and other rituals are held sharp to time and everything moves in an orderly manner.

The Devasthanam reminds one of the celebrated temple at Tirupathy in South India. The annual festival is usually held in August-September, culminating with the ratham festival, a day before the theertham, besides which there are several special festivals. Renovation is now in hand. A 71 ft. high Rajagopuram, depicting the ten incarnations of Vishnu and the history of the temple, will be erected.

Reference:

Pulavar Peethamparam (1819) has composed a garland of verses entitled 'Vallipuram Pathiham' (Tamil), later Sivasampoo Pulavar (1852-1910) also has offered to the Lord a pathiham of verses. The 1977 Kumba-Abishega Malar published by the new Trustee Board provides useful reading matter.

74. SRI RAMA BHAGAVAN'S SOJOURN IN LANKAPURAM

Mythology and tradition maintain that Sri Rama is an avatar of Maha Vishnu. The story of his sojourn in Lanka is therefore of relevant interest.

The story of the Ramayana epic is well known. Ravana, Emperor of Lankapuram abducted Sita Devi from the Dandaha forest in India and kept her in captivity in Lanka. Sri Rama Bhagavan arrived in Lankapuram with his vanara forces, vanquished Ravana and released his Queen Sita. Many places in Sri Lanka still retain lingering landmarks of this legendary episode.

The epic describes the expedient made to enable Sri Rama and his forces to cross the narrow water stretch (now known as Palk Straight) about 18 miles wide between the Indian continent and Lanka.

Though legendarily attributed to have been the handiwork of the vanara (monkey?) forces, parts of his bridge (or more likely embankment of rubble), however constructed, still survive sufficiently enough to obstruct navigation. Enjoying the dignified name of Adam's Bridge, it has been described (ref 1) as consisting 'of several paralled ledges of conglomerate and sandstone, hard at the surface and growing coarse and soft as it descends till it rests on a bank of sand'.

That is the present condition of the 'bridge' designed by Neelan, son of the immortal Maha Thuwadda, Architect of the Gods, and erected by denizens of the forest.

Villundi Theertham at Jaffna

In the heart of Jaffna Town is found the well known Villundi theertham. Today it consists of built up water tanks of sizes over a hundred feet long and of equal width. These are fed by fresh water spouts, which local folk-lore associates with Sri Rama Bhagavan. It is said that he originated this spring, by boring with his 'villu', to obtain water to quench the thirst of his forces. Jaffna however is a bit out of the way for visitation by an expeditionary task force marching to Lankapuram via Adam's Bridge. What ever that may be, there it is, a holy ghat at Villundi, with commemorative theertham and a well maintained Pillaiyar Kovil in its neighbourhood.

Ramalingeswaram

Rama Bhagavan's sojourn to Lanka is also perpetuated by his installation of a sacred Siva Lingam off Chilaw, as already mentioned.

Sri Rama Navami, the birthday of Sri Rama Bhagavan which occurs on the 9th (Navami) day of the month of Panguni, is observed at all the Vishnu and other temples, when excerpts from the Ramayana are read.

Reference:

1.   Raghavan, M. D., 'Tamil Culture in Ceylon', p. 48

75. KANNIYA (HOT SPRINGS) THEERTHA STHALAM OF VISHNU ORIGIN NEAR TRINCOMALEE:

Besides the Vishnu temple in Trincomalee; there is also a sthalam founded by Vishnu. The celebrated Kanniya theertha sthalam is situated a few miles to the west of Trincomalee on the Road to Anuradhapura. According to Puranams, it was divinely originated by Lord Vishnu. Ravana, while at Koneswaram, where he came for worship frequently, received the news of his mother's demise from Maha Vishnu who appeared as a Munivar. Ravana was stricken with grief. The Munivar consoling him advised that obsequies for the repose of his dead mother be performed at this spot selected by him. He probed the earth at seven places and a spring gushed out from each. Thus the seven wells of Kanniya came into being, with water of varying temperature gushing out from each, even today.

These have been built up as seven separate wells about a metre square and of equal height. The water in them never spills out, nevertheless refills even when drawn continuously. The water in each well is at a different temperature. On a day when the atmosphere was at 80°, the temperature of the water in each well was 107°, 105°, 101.5°, 101°, 91°, 88.5° and 86° respectively. Chemical analysis shows the presence of salts and nitrogen in the water. It is of course of therapeutic value found useful for rheumatism and skin ailments.

The site is frequented daily by pilgrims who come to perform their ablutionary bathing. With the Ravana legend, it is a frequented site for obsequies or last rites to the departed such as the asthi ceremonies. Madams for overnight residence and other facilities cater for the needs of every one, for, was it not this location selected by Maha Vishnu himself. There is a Vinayakar temple for worship.

Reference:

Somaskandar V. Pulavar and Sriskantha Raja A., 'Thiru-Koneswaram' (Tamil), 1963, pp 60-62

76. VISHNU TEMPLES IN BATTICALOA

Vishnu temples are a special feature in the Batticaloa region. As the eastern deltaic region abounds with natural pasture lands it is noted for breeding of cattle, and the availability of good supply of milk, curd and ghee. Some have attributed this factor to the prevalence of Vishnu Temples and Krishnan Kovils in the area, as Krishna is the patron of cow-herds. But more likely the existence of Vishnu temples, some of which are ancient, are due to their introduction during the era of King Kalinga Magha (1215-1255) later known in history as King Magha or Makone. He came from a part of India where reverence to Rama Bhagavan predominates and settling down, paid special attention for the development of the eastern regions of the island.

Whatever may have been the cause there are several Vishnu Kovils today in the Batticaloa region. The form of worship and the rituals observed at these are unique and are not prevalent elsewhere. (A tendency for change is however perceptible in recent years). The temples remain closed and the doors are opened only for the annual 'chadangu' or wedding festival. During the period of the festival, this generally lasts nine days, reading of the valourous deeds of Lord Krishna, such as in 'Kanchan Ammanai' forms the main item. Festivals are then held daily depicting exploits of Lord Krishna culminating with his wedding.

Some of the well known Vishnu Kovils of Batticaloa are those at Thimila Theevu, Vantharu Moolai, Kurukkal Madam, Kaluthavala, Kalladi, Karaitivu, Palukaman, and Thambilai Villu; of these the first two are reputed for holding elaborate annual festivals during which historic events are depicted in drama form.

77. DEHIWELA NEDUMAL VISHNU ALAYAM, COLOMBO

In the historical days, there is said to have been a Vishnu place of worship to the south of Colombo, the exact whereabouts of which are unknown. Today we have only the place name 'nedumale', given to a region east of the Dehiwela suburb of Colombo to remind us of the one time Vishnu worship here. Any temple of stone architecture could have been outstanding and referred to as 'Kal Kovil', which could easily become Kal Kovilu or Kalubowila, the present name of the locality. All this is of course only conjecture.

Whatever that may be, the story of the sacred Alayam of today to Maha Vishnu at Nedimale, off Anderson Road, Dehiwala has its beginnings in the 18th century.

A Vaishnavite devotee supervisor, engaged in the excavation of the Dutch canal near Dehiwela had a vision. He was told to seek a particular place, for his devotion to Lord Vishnu his patron, deity. He gave up his search in the jungle neighbouring Dehiwela after an initial attempt. However, the vision occurred again; so he set forth with a determination this time. Curiously, a young cow calf proceeded ahead of him and stopped at a particular spot in the jungle. To his amazement, the devotee found that it was a hallowed place. There were the ruins of a well and all the signs of a one-time Vaishnava Alayam, which had been eclipsed. Tulasi plants, sacred to the Lord flourished there. So a humble shed was commenced there and soon, votaries gathered there; persons bereft of progeny flocked there begging Vishnu for the gift of an offspring.

Among such, was one Arumugam unto him was born a son, whom the happy father decided to dedicate for services to the Lord. The infant was taken charge of by a sanniyasi, who, naming him 'Theeran' guided him as a Guru.

Theeran became very knowledgable in religious matters and soon earned the name of 'Theera swamy'. Going on pilgrimage to well known religious centres in S. India, he brought with him a celebrated Vel which he installed here for worship, and can be seen even today. About fifty years ago, I remember, the procession from this temple with the Vel, winding its way to Colombo city and back.

Present revival has been most striking. In 1971 interest in the temple was revived, and several additions and improvements were done and a grand Krishna Jayanthi celebrated in 1975. A notable event was the visit of a Vaishnavaite devotee, Mohan, a well to do merchant, who sponsored contact of the local temple management with the Thiruppathy sthalam in S. India. Vigraka murthies were obtained from that sacred Vishnu Alayam for installation here. On the 21st of January, 1983 was celebrated the divine nuptial of Venkadesa Nivasa Peruman with Pathmavathy Thayar.

This Vishnu Alayam in Colombo, situated in shady coconut grove, has now become to be venerated as a veritable Thiruppathy shrine in Eelam. It is comprehensive with many of the shrines found in a Vishnu sthalam. A small Vinayaka shrine with a Vel at the entrance leads to the sanctum, with the Boo Devi and Sri Devi shrines on either side.

Krishna deity is worshipped with his consorts in a separate shrine in the maha mandapam where there is also the Vishnu pada shrine. An impressive Sri Ranga Moorthy, in the syana pose, with attendants, is seen in the praharam. A Saniyeswaran and a naga thambiran shrines are found outside, in front. Regular pujas and festivals are meticulously observed.

Among the charitable undertaking here is the feeding of the poor, undertaken by the devotees.

Reference:

'Kumba abisheha malar', 1979, a Temple publication

78. RUINS OF VISHNU KOVILS

The Cholas when they were in Lanka, during the years 1017 to 1070 AC, had their capital at the ancient city of Pulasthipuram in Polonnaruwa, named by them as Janananatha Mangalam. Several Hindu temples had been erected there by them for the benefit of the Hindu community. Among these temples, the ruins of which are seen today, are not only Sivan Kovils, but also a few Vishnu Kovils. The statue of Lord Vishnu was found and unearthed in these temples when they were excavated by the Archaeological Department. Some of these are described below, but for a full description reference may be made to the relevant Annual Reports of the Archaeological Commissioner, published as Government Ses-sional Papers from the year 1901 onwards.

There had been, in all, apparently six separately erected Vishnu Kovils.

It has not been possible to trace much detail about the first Vishnu temple closest to the ancient city.

Second Vishnu Kovil, is at the northern entrance to the ancient city

This excellent temple is found in ruins at the northern entrance to the old city, opposite the ruins of a Sivan Kovil (Siva Devale No. 7) and a Vinayakar Kovil across the road. In a good state of presevation and of superior workmanship, it was first opened up in 1886 and the statue of Maha Vishnu, found at that time, is still seen in the sanctum, standing on its pedestal.

RUINS of Vishnu Temple, near the Northern entrance.

The entire temple had been of moulded granite stones and is approximately fifty feet long by twenty feet. The moolasthanam is about nine feet rectangular with a smaller artha mandapam opening out to a maha mandapam about twenty feet long, much of the excellent workmanship can be seen today.

As can be seen in the picture the basement of the entire structure has been raised about five feet high, the front facade of which is ornamented with central niches with supporting pillars. The lion frieze work on the stones, can be seen around the structure.

The structure has been sited with a road frontage and had to therefore face west; the theertham drains out from the sanctum northwards, unlike from its customary left side.

The Vishnu Murthi statue found in the Kovil is of granite, and is seen standing today on the original padmasana or lotus pedestal. It is three feet eight inches high; three arms bear the traditional emblems, the sakkaram the conch and the lotus; the fourth arm is lifted in abaya (blessing) pose.

Excavation and unearthing was done in the year 1907 and details appear in the annual report of the Archaeological Commissioner for that year.

In the earlier excavations, in 1887, other statues including those of Vinayakar, Subramaniar, Iswaran and others unidentified had been found.

Third Vishnu Kovil by the Tank

These ruins are by the tank and are seen by the road from Habarana, located opposite the ruins of Siva Devale No. 4 across the road. The granite pillars and the brickwork in the superstructure are clearly seen in the picture. The forty foot long temple structure had stood within a walled enclosure of about 150 ft. by 100 ft. The eight foot square moolasthanam is joined by an artha mandapam of equal size opening out to a 25 feet long maha mandapam.

In the debris was found the Maha Vishnu Murthi statue, finely carved in relief and about 3 ft. 9 inches high, bearing in three arms the traditional Vishnu emblems of the Sakkaram, the conch, lotus and the fourth arm is held high in abhayam (blessing) pose.

This was excavated in 1902 and is reported on Sessional Papers No. LX VII of 1907.

Fourth Vishnu Kovil, adjoining Siva Devale No 5

Standing side by side with Siva Devale No 5 on the road to Anaivulandava, can be seen the ruins of yet another Vishnu Kovil.

Like the neighbouring temple to Lord Siva, this Vishnu Kovil also had been more elaborate and was probably the biggest. Built in a walled enclosure about a hundred feet long, there had been a large garbagrakam over ten feet wide, in which is a neatly finished peedam or pedestal three feet square, visible in the picture. A smaller artha mandapam leads to a larger mandapam about fifteen feet long which is followed by a still bigger maha Mandapam, with rooms.

The site was first unearthed in 1908, and a long list of 'finds' is reported in the Commissioner's Annual Report, published as Sessional Paper No IV of 1913

Fifth Vishnu Kovil

About half a mile further along this road are seen the remnants of the ruins of an old Sivan Kovil, designated Siva Devale No 6. The Siva Lingam and Vinayaka Murthi statues, in it, can be seen highly weathered and stone flaked.

Ruins of Vishnu temple near Siva Devale 5

Just outside these ruins was unearthed the ruins of a small twenty foot shrine, in the mandapam of which was found a Statue of Vishnu in relief standing with his two Sakthies.

SECTION V

SAKTHI TEMPLES

79. VENERATION OF SAKTHI

'Oh Loving Mother! Thou art the Primal Energy. Thou hast two aspects, namely, the peaceful and terrible. Thou art modesty, gentleness, shyness, generosity, courage, forbearance and patience. Thou art Faith in the heart of devotees and generosity in noble people, chivalry in warriors and ferocity in tigers.

Salutations unto thee, Oh Mother supreme!'   *(Sivananda)*

The Divine Power of Lord Siva, Energy or Sakthi has been personified for veneration and worship as God-Mother. The concept of a Divine Mother is natural to the human; Her Forms are numerous. There are the all pervading creative active energy aspect, a peaceful and graceful aspect and a fearful powerful aspect.

Her Manifestations

As Parvathy, She is the Lady of the Mountains, as Uma She is praised as Light, as Sivakami She is the beloved of Lord Siva.

As Gowri, She is the auspicious Devi, good of all the Good, accomplishing all objectives and specially worshipped as the Devi who grants all gifts which her devotees request of her. It is in this Form that she reigns at Thiruketheeswaram Temple in Sri Lanka.

As Durga, meaning valour, she is a form or aspect of Maha Devi Ambal. Ambal took on this form at the behest of the Supreme Lord Parameswara to demonstrate to the world at large the overcoming and elimination of Ignorance and Arrogance personified in the legend of Mahuda or Mahisha.

Ancient tradition went further and personified the active energies of the gods of the Hindu Pantheon giving them names associating them with their respective gods, such as:

> Brahmi or Saraswathi associated with Brahma,
> Narayani or Lakshmi with Narayana,
> Maheswari or Yogeswari with Maheswara,
> Varahi with Varaha,
> Kaumeri with Kumaran,
> Indrani with Indra

Her many Forms and Names

The Manifestations of the Devi are countless. Her many attributes have inspired giving her numerous Forms and Names. The Devi Mahtmya, a well known composition of 700 mantras extols her as Maha Kali, Maha Lakshmi, and Maha Saraswathy. One hundred and eight names of the Devi are praised in the Matsya Purana. Three hundred names are cited in the Sri Lalitha Trisothi Namavali.

Her Manifestation as Ambal at several Temples in Sri Lanka

In one Form or another Sakthi is venerated in every Hindu Temple in Sri Lanka. However certain temples have acquired a long time tradition as especially auspicious for her worship. She is venerated as the Divine Consort of Lord Siva and invariably enthroned in a separate shrine at all the Sivan Temples:

She manifests as:

> Gowri Ambal at Thiruketheeswaram,
> Madumai Ambal at Koneswaram,
> Anguleswari Ambal at Naguleswaram,
> Vadivambikai Ambal at Muneswaram,
> Nallanayaki Ambal at Saddanther Kovil,
> Thaiyalnayaki Ambal at Vaitheeswaran Kovil,
> Sivakamy Ambal at Ponnambalavaneswaram

Ambal Temples

There are several temples in Sri Lanka dedicated for the worship of Ambal, where she is installed as the principal deity, in the sanctum. Some of the temples where she reigns supreme and bestows Grace are, as:

> Parameswary Ambal at Pt. Pdro and Punguduthivu temples
> Sivakami Ambal at Kondavil and Inuvil temples
> Sivakamasundari at Thirunelvely
> Manonmany Ambal at Nallur, Naranthanai, Nanthavil and Pungun-guduthivu temples
> Puvaneswary Ambal at Achchuvely, Suthumalai, Ellallai and Puthur temples
> Rajarajeswary Ambal at Pallai, Nayanmarkadu and Sirupiddy temples
> Kamachchi Ambal at Nachchimar Kovil and Neerveli temples
> Ilankai Nayaki Ambal at Nallur temple

In the pages that follow in this Section, it will be seen how the one Sakthi is being venerated in Sri Lanka, under various Names in some of the temples. But they are all Forms and attributes of the one central Maha Devi, the Divine Power of Siva-Sakthi.

AMBAL KOVILS

80. SIVAHAMY AMBAL KOVIL, INUVIL.

During the era of the Tamil Kings of Jaffna, tradition has it that the Inuvil region, situated only four miles north of Jaffna, was of as great prominence as was Nallur, the capital city. The region covered several of the neighbouring villages of today. A prominent personage settled in the locality by the Tamil Kings was Peravuriyar, a noble chief. He and his clan, who also came with him, were well known for their piety and religious fervour in their homeland in South India. The region flourished with many Hindu temples, most of them standing even today; there are the Karunakara Pillaiyar temple to the east, Pararajasekara Pillaiyar temple to the south, Segaraja Sekara Pillaiyar temple to the west and Pallappai Vairavar Kovil to the north. The Viswanathar Sivan Kovil at Karaikkal, close by, also invites historical investigation. The chieftains who succeeded the noble Peravuriyar, prominent among whom were Kalinga Rayan and Kailaiyananthan, maintained the religious tradition, so much so that the latter is remembered today by a temple called Ilanthari Kovil, after his nick-name.

Sivahamy Ambal Temple, Inuvil
Perpetuates the glorious cultural era of the Tamil Kings

Amidst such an environment was founded Sivahamy Ambal Kovil, along with, it is said, the accompanying Sivan temple and Bhairava temple. The suceeding years of early foreign domination of the country, had devastating effects on Hindu temples and by the 18th century only the Ambal Kovil survived. It is known that Ambal Kovils being 'Mathavin Kovils', were spared from destruction by foreigners in the 17th century. This Ambal Kovil had been immortalised by an incident of inspiration which occured during the life of a poet named Sinnathamby Pulavar, in about the year 1760.

At the Inuvil Ambal Temple, a pretty little madam, erected by the local folks, in memory of their Inuvai Pulavar, who immortalised the Ambal with his compositions.

This poet is usually referred to as Inuvai Sinnathamby Pulavar, to distinguish him from the Nallur Sinnathamby Pulavar, son of Villavaraya Mudaliyar, who lived in Nallur, about the same time.

Sinnathamby of Inuvai was a son of Sithampara Nathar and lived during the years 1658 to 1762, the later era of the Dutch regime in Ceylon. Those were the days of eminent poets like Ganapathi Iyer (1709 -1784), Mylvagana Pulavar (1770 - 1867), and the Nallur poet (1716 - 1780). Young Inuvai was of humble origin and was moderately educated; but he was a born poet by nature.

A unique event in his life occured when he was accused of a false charge which he had never committed and was locked up. Furious, but with indomitable courage and unsevering faith to Sivahamy Ambal, he sang a pathikam of verses beseeching her aid. As he came to the 8th verse, Divine power opened the locks and he walked out a free man, to the consternation of every one and establishing his innocence.

From that day onwards, he became famous and continued with his compositions. Very soon he earned the honorific title of 'Kalthirkama Sekara Manu Mudaliyar', consequent to his writings and poetic compositions.

Among his works are:
1) Sivahamy Ammai Pillaithamil
2) Panchavarana thoothu and dramatic works:
3) Nondy Nadakam
4) Kovalan Nadakam
5) Aniyiritha Nadakam

Sivahamy Ambal Kovil thus gains prominence in our cultural and religious history.

The progeny of the early settlers continue to manage its affairs. Today we revere the Ambal Murtham in the Mulasthanam. A Raja Rajeswari Vigrakam is taken out in procession during festivals. The Nadarajah Murthi shrine is adjoining, facing south. In the prahara are shrines for Vinayakar Subramanya and Bahirava. There is also a Navagraha shrine.

The annual Mahotsava festivals are held in March, terminating with water cutting on Panguni uthiram.

Among the other festivals observed, the Adi Puram in July is a very special occasion when devotees from all over gather there for performance of their vows, by circumambulating the Devi, with lit camphor in pots. The Thiruvemba observance at dawn in December is well patronised by the agricultural population who proceed for work, thereafter.

Recently a new attractive Gopuram was erected, seen in the picture and a new Ther (temple chariot), was constructed in 1978.

'For all Devi's Grace is boundless'.

Reference:

1.   'Sivahamy Amman Kovil, Chithira Ther Thirappany Sirappu Malar 1978'; a Temple Publication

2.   'Senthamil Poompukall', part III, 1949 by Pandit A. S. Nagalingam

3.   'Elathu Thamil Kavithai Kalanchiyam', 1966, p. 46, compiled by Prof. A. Sathasivam

81. KAMADCHI AMBAL KOVIL VANNARPANNAI, JAFFNA
(Nachchimar Amman Kovil)

Sri Kamadchi Ambal is the patron deity of the Visva Kula gold merchants and craftsmen. In the ancient sacred puranams is found the story of Ambal Devi's ashdasda leelas as narrated by Soothai Maha Munivar to his disciples. Sri Kanchi Kamadchi Devi is one of the forms of the Devine. Ambal Devi regained her golden lustre and celebrated the event with a divine nuptial wedding, in the month of 'panguni'.

How Kamadchi Ambal became to be the presiding deity at this temple is of divine interest. In the olden days this location had a sequestered setting amidst clusters of cool shady 'naval' and 'Marutha' trees situated adjoining tank and paddy fields. The site 'Kularkarai Maruthadi' had, from time immemorial been notable for the veneration of 'amman'. It is said that one day a young lady polluted the place and suffered for it by having one of her breasts torn off from her. Whatever that may have been, the incident caused holy reverence to the spot and some one perpetuated it by installing a stone, citing it for worship of Nachchimar Amman, prevalent then. The location soon became a temple for regular worship and with a Mari Amman deity.

Eventually, the residents in the neighbourhood decided to install a Kanchi Kamadchi Vigraham, their patron deity.

It was then that one of their senior reverential personage by the name of K. Vaithilinga Pathar, going on pilgrimage to Sivasthalams in India, came in contact with a celebrated Kannaiyah Achchariyar. The Achchariyar, who was a very able sculpture artist, entrusted the pathar with an exquisite bronze Vigrakam statue of Kamadchi Ambal, created by him very specially, using all the experience of his ripe old age. This Vigrakam was brought and installed here in this temple, and given the name of Sri Kanchi Kamadchi Ambal Alayam. For casual purposes however, the old name of Nachchimar Kovil and Nachchimar Koviladi for the locality, are still in use.

The temple is very well maintained. Pujas are performed regularly and good administration is very evident. The annual Mahotsava festival is held for 15 days in March - April. Several other festivals are observed right through the year.

A new Ther chariot was constructed only a few years ago, a magnificent Rajagopuram was nearing completion when I went to make my obeisance to Ambal, early in 1982.

Temples dedicated to the worship of Kamadchi Ambal are also found at Neerveli and other places.

82. MEENADCHI AMMAN KOVIL, UDUVIL

The traditional pre-eminent Meenadchi Ambal temple is in the city of Mathurai, South India. There she reigns supreme with Lord Sunderaswarar. The puranams narrate the story of the divine nuptial of Supreme Parameswara as Sundaresan with Meenadchi, the daughter of the Pandyan King of Mathurai.

Temples dedicated for worship of Meenadchi Ambal are not many in Sri Lanka. At Uduvil, a hamlet, about six miles north of Jaffna, there is divine Amman Kovil, reached by the lane close to the well known Girl's School. The location is amidst the agricultural hinterland of the Jaffna Peninsula, surrounded by paddy fields. The origin of this Ambal temple is illuminating.

It is said that about a few hundred years ago at the time when land was being cleared for development, a stone, which was unique, was found at a particular place. At that spot, there was instituted a holy place and with the stone, a temple was founded for reverence to Kannakai Amman. About three hundred years ago, one Rangunatha Iyer erected a proper agamic temple here, installing an Ambal Vigrakam, dedicating the temple to Meenadchi Amman. His successors and progeny continue to administer the Kovil well.

Other Meenadchi Ambal Temples

There is also a Meenadchi Ambal Kovil at Achchuvely. In Pungudutivu West, we have a Meenahchi Ambal Sametha Sunderaswarer temple. The Madaththady Meenahchi Ambal temple at Batticaloa is said to be of ancient origin.

At Mahiyapiddi, in the outskirts of Kanterodai, there is an Anganammai temple housing both a Meenadchi Ambal and a Kannakai Amman deity. All Ambal festivals and pujas are observed there.

83. NAGA POOSHANIAMBAL KOVIL, NAINATIVU

Antiquarians have established the occupation of the Northern region by Nagas in the ancient days. Many customs, traditions and forms of worship still prevail which are attributed to them.

Veneration of the cobra or serpent worship has been an ancient custom. In due course, it is surmised, evolved the Hindu worship of Nagathambiran, when the Siva Linga deity is canopied by the hood of a five headed cobra, and Naga pooshani Ambal worship when the Ambal Devi is similarly exalted. A foremost sannithanam of this form of the Ambal, also known as as Nagambal or Nages-wari, is at Nainativu.

Nagapooshani Ambal Kovil, Nainativu

Nainativu, also referred to as Nagatheevu or Nagadeepa, is a small island of 4 square miles, off the Jaffna Peninsula. It had however enjoyed a foremost place in Lanka's history, having been the seat of the Naga Kingdom. Having several names: Nagathivu, Nainarthivu, Nagatheepam, Manithivu and Manipallavam, the location has been foremost in religious worship. That Bharata Prince Arjunan married Princess Sithirangai daughter of Sithiravakanan, the Naga king of Manipallavam, is a Maha Bharatham tradition. Naga kings are also said to have been dwelling in ancient Kanterodai, Nagarkovil, Matoddam and Kelaniya. Some of its ancient lore may also be read in the 'Manimekalai' an old time Tamil composition. Tradition strongly associates the island as having been visited by Kannakai and Manimekalai, sometime in their illustrious lives, thus associating veneration of Ambal Devi and the island.

Stories of early temples at this venerable Naga sthalam commences with the miracles observed by two traders Manayakan and Mahasathavan. They witnessed to their amazement a Naga serpent swimming in the sea towards this isle with a flower and what is more a vulture, was poised overhead. When the vulture was chased away, the serpent continued its journey for veneration of the divine at Nageswaram.

Two stones in the sea are pointed out, even today, as being the stones behind which the snake sheltered and the one where the vulture perched. The two traders founded a temple here and dedicated it to Ambal; it was later rebuilt as a grand temple with seven praharams by one Veerasami Chettiyar, housed with Ambal and Siva deities. But this edifice was demolished by the Portuguese along with other Hindu temples in 1620. The Ambal Vigrakam, it is said, was however saved from the demolishers and kept hidden in the trunk of a tree and venerated unostentatiously. In the eras of the revival of Hinduism, spearheaded by Arumuga Navalar a proper agamaic temple was erected in .1882 and the Ambal Devi Vigrakam installed with the name of Naga Pooshani Amman Kovil. Regular worship ensued and several improvements were effected by various devotees. A Rajagopuram was erected in 1935. The management of the affairs of the temple came under a Trustee Board in 1949.

A magnificent Ther chariot, said to be one of the best in Sri Lanka, was constructed for Ambal in 1957.

The main entrance to the temple and the sanctum face the east and the vast ocean, with a landing pier. The pilgrims, even as they land in the island pay obeisance to the Ambal. The figure of a five headed Naga serpent, is seen in the sanctum bearing the Ambal Devi's thiru uruvam. Even as we circumambulate along the prahara, we revere the figures of Durga Devi and Saptha matha seen on the niches of the sanctum walls.

In the inner praharam are shrines for Vinayakar and Subramaniyar, The Navagraha Kudu and shrines for Bhairavar, the Sun and the Moon are in their traditional locations.

The annual festival which lasts for fifteen days is a grand affair when thousands throng this little islet to receive Ambal's Grace. On other days, all the Hindu Saiva festivals are observed throughout the year. Daily regular pujas are performed four times.

No story of Nainativu is complete without the mention of its outstanding saintly personality 'Nainativu Swamiyar'. Born as Muthukumaraswamy, he became a great Gnani and attained higher realms of saintlyness, before his demise in 1949. His samadhi is a place of veneration in this isle.

There have been several compositions published at various times by several authors and pulavars, extolling ambal's Grace to her devotees.

Reference:

1.   Kula Sabanathan, 'Nayainai Nageswari' 1962 (Tamil)

2.   Shanmuganathapillai N. K. 'Purathari Nayinai Nagabooshini' 1981 (Tamil)

84. SEERANI NAGA POOSHANI AMBAL KOVIL, SANDILIPAI

Another foremost Naga Pooshani Ambal Kovil is at Seerani, Sandilipai, about 8 miles from Jaffna. Large numbers of devotees gather here for Ambal's tharisanam, particularly on the full moon day in April, when the Ther or the temple chariot Festival is celebrated.

The present phase of the story of Seerani Nagambal Kovil commences with Shanmuganathar Murugesapillai, who lived about a century ago. He was an illustrious descendant of Kula Nayaga Mudalaiyar and Punithivalla Mudaliyar, celebrated early settlers, who originally arrived from Karaikkal. Young Murugesapillai was a very pious person of quiet disposition who spent his time reading the puranas, reciting prayers and was specially devoted to the veneration of Ambal Devi. He happened to retrieve a 'Yantra' plate inscribed with mantras and ever since then Devi would frequent his dreams, asking him to erect a shrine for her veneration. Limited resources however prevented him from embarking on any such venture. However, on the night of the full moon day in April 1896, a particular location was pointed out to him to excavate and when he did that, to his great amazement he unearthed a bronze vigrakam, He was overjoyed, Ambal's grace was now unmistakable. Sakthi's divine energy inspired him to action and with hardly any funds he commenced building an Ambal Kovil, which grew, with support received from everywhere. Thus was commenced construction of this celebrated temple in the year 1896, and first pujas performed on Adi Amavasai, new moon day in July, auspicious for Devi.

Seerani Nagapooshani Ambal Temple.
Devotees at the Ther - car Festival, 1982

Commencing thus in a humble way, subsequent ample support enabled the building of a proper agamic temple structure and the observation of regular pujas and festivals.

In course of time when enthusiasm waned, the formation on 10 October 1962 of a Temple Thiruppani Sabai, widely spreadout in membership brought new sphere of temple activities.

Renovations were done on a large scale. The Maha Mandapam, Vasantha Mandapam, Yaga Salai, Kodi Sthampam were all repaired and improved, the beautiful statues depicting Ambal Devi's various activities seen on the sthoopy were all renewed. The Pirahara Murthi Shrines were also renovated.

A further land mark was the erection of a Ther, contributed by a devoted K. Thambiah and completed by his widow. This Ther chariot won the praise of all Jaffna for its superb construction and beauty of execution.

In the prakaram, we find today the shrines of Vinayaka, Subramanya and Bhairva Murthies. There is also the Navagraha Shrine.

An able line of 'Pathukavalars' have been looking after various affairs of the temple. Regular Pujas are performed six times daily; besides isolated festivals, the major Mahotsava festival is in April. Navarathiri Pujas are observed quite elaborately.

Legendary

For the bronze vigrakam to have been there, for pious Murugesapillai to unearth, the location had very likely been a place of Ammaiyar worship earlier; even centuries before. In this connection, the many places that Kannakai Amman stayed on her epic journey from Nainativa to Vaththapallai may be remembered. Each one of them is said to have become a place of sacred Amman worship.

Reference:

'Thiruppani Sabai Malar' (1963), Temple publication

Other Naga Pooshani Ambal Kovils:

There is another Naga Pooshani Ambal Kovil at Araly South, which also is associated by tradition, as a stopping place of Kannakai Amman. Similar temples are found at Kondavil and Navaly in the Jaffana peninsula. They are also found in the Mullaitivu and Batticaloa Districts.

DURGA DEVI KOVILS

Durga means Valour and Durga Devi is a form or aspect of Uma or Parvati Ambal. According to Hindu mythology, Ambal took on this form at the behest of supreme Parameswara, to demonstrate to the world at large the overcoming and elimination of ignorance and arrogance personified in legends as Mahuda or Mahisha Asuran.

The story is that an arrogant munivar, by name Varan, incurred the displeasure of Agasthiya Maha Munivar and had to languish as an Asura with a buffalo's head, the symbol of ignorance and arrogance. Mahudasuran in his arrogance spread a reign of terror in the Mysore region. He illtreated everyone and persecuted the Devas who had to seek refuge. Ambal Devi, as Durga, with powers gained from thapas at Arunachchalam, first vanquished his generals Chandan and Mandan, thereby becoming known also as Chamundi. She then overcame the asuran himself and eliminated all that he personfied. Her apperarance is made impressive by being portrayed with ten arms, indicative of her power over the ten quarters - the eight quarters of the universe, the heavens above and the nether world below. She carries the trident of the Supreme One as armour and is often depicted engaged in combat, with a lion beneath her and about to maul the asura. Symbolically Durga depicts elimination of ignorance and deliverance from illusion.

Among the several festivals, we observe, invoking Sakthi, the energy of the supreme one, the Navarathiri nine day festival is most auspicious. Durga Devi is invoked during the first three nights, Lakshmi on the second three nights and Saraswathy during the last three nights. The observance is often spoken of as Saraswathy puja because it concludes with it.

The tenth day of this observance is equally important. It is Vijaya Dasami day or the day of Victory. It is on this day that Sakthi, as Durga Devi overcame the forces of ignorance, portrayed as Mahudasuran, referred to above. Festivals are held in temples in which Devi is shown wiping out ignorance by the cutting into pieces branches of a tree or a plantain stem. The Vanni tree, in which the asuran sought refuge towards the end, is much sought.

The Dasaratha festival used to be observed on a most lavish scale at Mysore, during the era of the Maharajah's rule.

In Bengal, where Sakthi worship predominates, the Durga puja is their greatest national festival.

TEMPLES

There are not many temples dedicated to the worship of Durga Devi in Sri Lanka. A foremost temple is at Tellipalai in Jaffna, where large congregations gather.

At Thalaiyadi, a village off Nunavil junction near Chavakachcheri is a Devi temple, more often known as just 'Thalaiyadi Amman Kovil'. It is beautifully located among 'thalai' bushes adjoining paddy fields. Though small it is complete with traditional prahara murthi shrines for Pillaiyar, Skanda and Bhairavar. Saniyeswara Murthi is also installed but in a separate shrine. Many of the buildings have been renovated and regular puja ceremonies established.

Durga Devi temples are also found at Nunavil, and Elalai.

Reference:

'Durga Devi Valipadu' (Tamil) by S. Kanapathipillai 1981

A Vanni Tree at Punnalai Temple: This is traditionally associated with the mythological overcoming of Mahista Asuran by Durga Devi.
The author making enquiries

85. DURGA DEVI KOVIL, TELLIPALLAI

A Durga Devi Kovil, where thousands of devotees congregate daily, is Devi's Devasthanam at Tellipallai, about 8 miles north of Jaffna on the road to Kankesanturai; all roads lead to Tellipallai on Tuesdays, the auspicious day for Devi worship.

Durga Devi temple, Tellipallai, Jaffna

Although this temple has become prominent in recent years, it has an old history. It is said that about four hundred years ago, a venerable devotee by the name of Kathirkamar had gone on pilgrimage to India; there he worshipped at several Hindu holy sthalams, Benaras, Mathurai and Rameswaram. On his return, arriving at Kankesanturai he had walked a few miles when he felt tired and rested by the wayside. Durga desired that to be her location. So he installed the Sakthi Yantra which he had carefully brought from Benaras, there under an 'Illupai' tree, thus commencing worship, which is to become an outstanding Devi Sthalam.

The location soon became a place of reverence to the Devi and the temple assumed shape by 1829 when the first Kumba abishekam was performed. Pujas were performed by priests from Kanchipuram. Management was under Udaiyar Kathirasar Pillai and his heirs. In 1953 the temple Trustee Board launched a building campaign and a proper agamic temple structure was completed and Kumba abishekam ceremonies held in 1965. Additions and improvements are being carried out, now with the provision of several mandapams and madams. Spacious madams permit devotees to observe charitable deeds such as feeding the poor.

In the praharam there are temples for Pillaiyar, Gaja Lakshmi Murukan and Bhairaver. The Gaja Lakshmi shrine attracts special attention of the devotees who perform rites to invoke aid from the Devi.

The Devi deity is serene and calm. The utsava deity faces south.

A prominent personality in the service of the Devi is the distinguished Thangamma Appukutty, well known for her scholarship and learning in Hindu religious matters. Her devotion and tireless service has uplifted Devi's temple to a premier Hindu Thevasthanam of today.

Daily, all the pujas are performed meticulously. Several Devi observances are held throughout the year.

Regular annual mahotsava festivals were commenced in 1968 and are observed in August. A temple Ther chariot was completed in 1978 for the festival. Recently a Raja Gopuram was erected at the entrance and Kumba Abishekam performed in 1981.

Reference:

'Maha Kumba Abisheka Malar', 1981, a temple publication

KALI AMMAN KOVILS

Kali Devi is conceived as an aspect, a power aspect, of Uma or Parvati Ambal. She is often personified as dark, violent and valourous. We see her portrayed in her fierce aspect combating Darukasuran, a wicked asuran, whom she destroys with flames. In this posture she is seen mounted on a lion, with the attendant flames behind and holding a trisoolam. According to a boon enjoyed by the asuran, he cannot be destroyed in battle or combat. So the Kali Devi aspect utilised fire to burn him up. She gets her name, Kali, from the mode of her creation.

She figures in several of the legends of Hindu mythology. In some myths we find her personality bifurcating into two, one a dark and fierce Bhadra Kali and the other a golden, serene pleasant Swarna Valli. The latter is said to have merged with Uma Ambal.

Thillai Kali legend is the story of her 'Nadiyum' contest with Lord Siva, in which she is subdued to become benevolent and is subsequently given a place within the temple.

Whatever all these stories may be, worship of Kali Devi is very popular and we find her vigrakam in almost all Sivan Kovils and in other temples as well. She is generally installed in a separate shrine or niche and we have her tharisanam as we circumambulate the inner prahara of the temple; she is usually bedecked with Kunkumam and a red garment.

It may be because of the skill and valour depicted in the form that worship of Kali Devi is particularly propitious to those engaged in skilled professions and vocations. She is the patron deity of the artist, sculptor, the sthapathy and all craftsmen; they revere her as Veerama Kali. Veeramakali temples are found at Nallur, Inuvil, and Kerutadavil.

Evidence has been found of the prevalence of reverence to the Devi in ancient times. In fact, it has been said that Siva and Kali were the most popular deities venerated by the ancient Hindus.

Some have surmised that Kali worship emanated from worship of Mother Goddess, known to have been an ancient cult, as Sakthi worship. Even in recent years Swami Ramakrishna Paramahamsa of Calcutta and India's national poet Subramaniya Bharatiyar were especially devoted to the worship of Kali Devi.

KALI DEVI TEMPLES

In Sri Lanka, the Devi is revered as benevolent mother Sakthi, the protector and guardian of her peoples. Bhadra Kali Amman temples are usually sited at the entrance to the village, from where the Devi safeguards (Kaval) the village from asuras. Her worship was once associated with animal sacrifice, but that is now no more.

Some of the foremost of Devi's temples visited by me and where I have worshipped are described in the ensuing pages. Besides these, Bhadra Kali Amman temples are found at:

Thirunelvely, Achchuvely, Chulipuram, Thumpalai, and Vannarponnai in Jaffna.
At Mullaitivu, Kalmunai and Mandapaththady in Batticaloa.
There may be several others as well.

86. KALI DEVI KOVIL, KANNATHIDDI, VANNARPANNAI, JAFFNA

A small but beautiful temple housing Kali Devi is found at Kannathiddi, a few minutes walk from Vaitheeswara Sivan Kovil at Vannarpannai. In fact it is said that the Kali Kovil was built for worship by the many sthapathy artists and sculptors who were recruited by Vaithilinga Chettiyar from India for the construction of the Sivan Kovil, about the year 1782. The Chettiyar was a benevolent personality. A fine lotus pond across the road provides a beautiful setting, where I always stop and rest for a while, when I pass that way (that was in the nineteen twenties).

Kannathiddy Kali Amman Kovil, Jaffna
Entrance off the main road

The temple was later renovated and rebuilt in 1800 by the Vishvakula gold craftsmen and merchants, Sponsored by the many 'pather' families and others of the locality. Further improvements were effected in 1918 and later in 1940 and 1970.

Created, for the worship of their patron deity, by master craftsman whose vocation was to build temples and ornament them, the temple is a small masterpiece in masonry. An imposing Kali Devi presides in the moolasthanam and the traditional prahara murthies adorn the temple.

The highly decorated Sthoopi, of Kannathiddy Kovil

Regular pujas are performed four times daily. The 21 day Gowri fast is observed with special ceremonies. The Navrathiri nine day observance is a very special occasion when elaborate festivities are held for 15 days.

A Kumba Abishekam ceremony was held in 1971.

87. BHADRA KALI AMMAN KOVIL, PIDDIYAMPATHY, SANGARATHAI

At Sangarathai, a hamlet about 8 miles from Jaffna there is a Bhadra Kali Kovil situated amidst vast paddy fields. The location is easily reached as the road from Anaikoddai passes by the site.

The origin of this Kovil is an interesting tradition. About 300 years ago, a leading resident of the place observing that the large, spreading tamarind tree growing at this spot was harmful to paddy cultivation, decided to do away with it. There were workmen engaged in building work at that time (1678) at neighbouring Vaddukoddai. They however refused to fell this tree, for fear. The tree already had a holy association. So the irate resident started setting about felling it himself, when Lo! There came a cobra from the tree and chased him off and he had to flee. That night Kali Devi, in a dream besought him to erect a shelter for her there. He forthwith got erected a humble shed by the side of the tree, which in course of time has been built up as a proper temple structure.

Bhadra Kali Amman Kovil, Sangarathai

Now large mandapams and halls adorn the structure and several improvements have been added. A very large theertha kerney (tank) with build-in steps adorn the front. In the prahara is a shrine for Vinayakar and a separate outside shrine for Bhairava Murthi.

The ancient tamarind tree stands there by the side of the sanctum and is much venerated by the local Sangarathai folks. Pujas are also performed at the shrine beneath, venerating it as Veerapathirar mandapam. It is the link with the past.

A special feature at this temple is the installation of Virapathirar Murthi and Kali Devi as presiding deities in the sanctum. The significance of this alludes to an event in Hindu mythology. Thakkan, who at one time had received divine powers from supreme Parameswara, had become drunk with that power and was performing yagnas against Him and had to be overcome. So, it is said, Siva created Veerapathirar, and Ambal created Bhadra Kali to overcome Thakkan. Thakkan was eventually subdued by them. Veerapathirar Swamy and Bhadra Kali Devi are considered as personification of the Grace of Lord Siva and Ambal Devi. This aspect is illustrated in this temple dedicated to Bhadra Kali Ambal Sametha Veerapathirar Swamy.

Many devotees of Sangarathai have contributed liberally for the renovation and building work making it an excellent structure. Prominent among them who laboured are Rasanayagam Trustee and Vairavanathar, retired school master. The younger generations of the locality are enthusiastic devotees and no 'Thakkan' can dare any harm to them.

Regular pujas are performed and many of the other Hindu festivals also observed here. The annual festival which lasts for ten days is held in March, after the paddy has been harvested.

Reference:

'Bhadra Kali Ambal Sametha Veerapathira Swamy story and Unjal songs' (Tamil) 1971, - a temple publication

88. VEERA MAKALI AMMAN KOVIL, SARASALAI

At Sarasalai, a village a few miles from Chavakachcheri is found another Amman kovil dedicated to the worship of Veera Makali Devi. It commenced from humble origins.

About a few hundred years ago there lived a venerable person named Kathiravelar. He is known to have travelled on pilgrimage to several Hindu sthalas in India. Once he brought with him a divine small Kali Devi statue from Chidambaram (Thillai). Placing it beneath a naval tree, at the site of the present temple, he instituted regular worship of this Thillai Kali Devi. Soon a structure was erected here.

Much building work remains to be done to complete the structure to a proper temple. In the sanctum is a large and impressive Kali Devi Vigrakam. Prahara temples and mandapams are under erection. A special shrine in the prahara houses the old Thillai Kali Devi which the local folks devotedly adore even today.

89. BHADRA KALI AMMAN KOVIL, TRINCOMALEE

In Trincomalee town is found a well-known Bhadra Kali Amman Kovil; it is said to have an ancient history associated with the Kulakoddan era of Konesar temple. The people of Trincomalee revere her as the guardian deity of the city; she is fondly referred to as 'Nagara Kali'.

The temple structure that we see today at this venerated ancient location was rebuilt in 1933 and subsequently improved in 1947, with the addition of maha mandapam. So that we have today a temple structure errected in keeping with the traditional requirements complete with bell-tower and east-facing main entrance. Artistic pillars and decorative walls and mandapams adorn the temple.

A very impressive large Kali Devi deity installed in the sanctum, presides majestically bestowing her graceful protection to the Trincomalee folks.

They are greatly devoted to their custodian deity and gather at the temple daily beseeching the Devi's grace.

In the praharam are shrines for Vinayakar, Subramaniyar, Nagathambiran and Bhairavar.

Regular pujas are performed by the priests, who for generations have been looking after the affairs of the temple.

The annual festivals are held for ten days in the month of March culminating with a ther (car) festival when three ther chariots are towed circumambulating the Kovil.

The nine day Navarathiri festival in October is elaborately observed, extolling the Devi's divine powers. The succeeding 21 day, Kethara Gowri observance has been a special popular feature of this temple. A special festival on the last day releases the devotees of the 21 day fast observed by them.

A lavish Kumba abishekam ceremony was recently held in 1980.

Reference:

1,   Kumba Abisheham Malar, published by the Temple authorities

2.   Two ancient compositions in Tamil, titled: 'Pathira Kali Amman, Pathiham and Kali Vemba', collected & published by S. A. Kandiah of Colombo 6 in 1974.

90. VEERA MAHA KALI AMMAN KOVIL, NALLUR, JAFFNA

A temple where I used to play in my young days in the outer praharas is the Veera Maha Kali Amman Kovil at Nallur West, Vannarponnai. Located by the Point Pedro Road, it is hardly a mile from the heart of Jaffna town. For me, the outstanding annual event is Maha Kali Amman's all-night procession, in a 'thandikai' around Nallur.

It was for the purpose of safe-guarding his little kingdom, that Kalinga Singai Ariyan, the first Ariya Chakravarti King of Jaffna, founded this temple. As said earlier a temple was erected in each of the four directions around the city of Nallur. The name of Kanakacuriam who reigned for a long period as Pararaja Sekaram, King of Jaftna, is also associated with these four temples, as having improved them.

Kali Amman's blessings for success are specially invoked by many before they embark on dangerous or risky operations. Here, it is said, the soldiers would assemble and swear their oaths of fidelity and have their swords blessed by Kali Devi, before they go to the battlefield. Her blessings are auspicious, even today, for use of all tools and implements by the artisans.

Veera Maha Kali Amman Temple, Nallur
Kali's blessings are sought before undertaking hazardous undertakings

The temple was the scene of an unfortunate historical incident in the sixteenth century. Sangili was king of Jaffna, reigning as Sega Raja Sekaram from 1519-1564. At a time when he was hard pressed by the Portuguese there came to his aid Vidiya Bandara, a general who had fallen out with the Portuguese. An agreement was soon reached between Sangili and Vidiya Bandara against the Portuguese, their common enemy and to vouchsafe their contract they assembled before the Veera Kali Amman temple to swear their oath of fidelity; unfortunately an explosion that had taken place at a neighburing ammunition store caused a commotion in which Vidiya Bandara was killed. Sangili very much regretted this incident and it is said that he erected the Pootharayar Temple at Nallur as expiation, in memory of his friend.

The location was also the battlefield in the 'eleven day seige' of Nallur, in the war between Sangili and the invading Portugnese, according to the Yalpana Vaipava Malai. In the battle that took place in 1560, Sangili was victorious. He, however, lost later and was captured.

The temple was destroyed by the invaders, in the year 1621 along with other temples.

The present temple that is seen in the picture was built when Hinduism was resuscitated in the Arumuga Navalar era, near the site of the original temple. The Annual festival lasts 25 days, finishing with the full moon day in June. There is the annual outing, referred to earlier, when Kali Devi makes her ceremonial procession or 'urvalam' around Nallur.

The residents receive her with the traditional 'mandahapady' at their entrances. The boys enjoy a feed of vadais and other short eats at each of them. All this provides a feeling of security to the Nallur folks. They feel confident that Devi's tharisanam safeguards them against all form of epidemics, infectious diseases and other afflictions.

Reference:

Sinnathamby Pulavar (1830-1878) has composed a pathiham of verses (Tamil) on the Ambal Devi.

MUTHUMARI AMMAN KOVILS

Worship of Mari Amman and Muthumari Amman is largely prevalent in this country. Almost every village in the north and the east has its Mari Amman temple in the outskirts. Among the reasons adduced is that reverence to Muthu Mari Amman thwarts occurrence of pestilence, infectious diseases and smallpox in particular, among the community. It is somewhat difficult to ascertain how this belief got established.

Mythology portrays her being a creation of the holy trinity Brahma, Vishnu and Lord Siva for exterminating a demon asura who was persecuting the Devas. The Mari cult takes many names Mari, Muttumari and Mahamari, to whom the people turned for succour when stricken with infectious diseases.

The word 'Mari' denotes something cool or soothing as is the rainy season after the hot spell. Very often her worship is propitiated with margosa leaves - useful to disinfect and ward off and scare away harmful insects. A popular ritual is the 'karakam' ritual in which a pot of unguents with margosa leaves is ceremoniously conveyed with music and dancing to the Amman Kovil.

There have however, been notable changes. No longer is Amman's temple a neglected or haunted spot. Most of the Mari Amman temples have been opened up and enlarged. We now find housed in them the traditional deities of the Hindu pantheon, Sivan, Parvati and others. Higher forms of reverence and worship have been adopted and undesirable practices such as animal sacrifice abandoned. Brahmin priests now officiate and agamic rituals and ceremonies are adopted. In practice worship of Muthumari Amman is now more or less identifiable with worship of Ambal Devi.

There are a large number of Amman temples in Sri Lanka, one can easily count over a hundred Mari Amman and Muthumari Amman temples. Some of them such as the one at Kotahena, Colombo are very popular where large number of worshippers congregate to revere the Devi.

Some of these are described in detail in the ensuing pages besides which there are of course several others. At Perumkulam, Velanai is an ancient Mari Amman temple, the structure of which always reminds me of the Nagapooshani Ambal Kovil at Nainativu.

At Kaladdy, Vannarponnai is a well attended Amman temple.

The Nawalapitiya temple is well known and well-frequented for worship by devotees from the hill - country region.

There is a Mari Amman Kovil at Angana Ammai Kadavai, Mahiyapiddi besides the ambal kovils; these three originated from a vision of three maidens who sought solace there.

91. MUTHUMARI AMMAN KOVIL, KOPAY

At Kopay, about six miles from Jaffna, is situated a serene small Muthumari Amman temple amidst vast paddy fields. Commencing as a Nachchimar temple by a celebrated personage of the locality, this humble shrine is being rapidly built up as a proper Amman Kovil. The Amman Vigraham in the moolasthanam is in a seated position facing east. The utsava moortham is found in the south facing shrine.

Surrounded by walls, the temple with its mandapams, bell tower and prahara, enjoys a quiet environment under the shelter of a large tree. It has its Vinayaka, Subramaniya shrines within and the Bhairava Murthi shrine outside.

Muthumari Amman Kovil, Kopay

The congregation consisting of enthusiastic devotees celebrates and observes all the Hindu festivals propitious to the Amman, including an annual procession around Kopay in March. Full moon days are observed with a special festival and feeding of the poor. One simha vahanam majestically serves all festivals.

Though not an ancient temple, its location is associated with the regime of the Kings of Jaffna, when there was a fort and stronghold at Kopay for their retreat. Relics and heirlooms of the royalty may be discovered one day in the neighbourhood. But the faithful devotees of Kopay are blessed with Ammaiyar's Grace. They contribute towards the management of the temple.

92. MUTHUMARI AMMAN KOVIL, VALVETTITURAI

It is not often that we see a Muthumari Amman temple erected by the side of a Sivan Temple. However, so it is, at Valvettiturai, at Thirunelvely Nallur, the Muthumari Amman Kovil is close to the Tirunelvely Sivan Kovil, but across the roadway.

Religious establishments in this area are traditionally associated with the days when Karunakara Thondaiman, a distinguished general under King Kulatunga Cholan I (1070 -1118. AC), came to Jaffna to manufacture and export salt to his home country. His name is also associated with founding of Hindu temples. Then it was the Chola era, the days of Glory to Hinduism. In any case, Valvetiturai would have figured for attention by the Kings of Jaffna in their communication with the Kings of Mathurai in South India, across the straits.

Historically, it is said to have been built or restored during the era of revival of Hinduism, about the year 1795.

A delightful story narrated about its origin is that of an old woman who had demanded passage to Valvettiturai, from boatmen plying from S. India to this place. Coercing them to take her, she travelled and disembarking at Valvetiturai disappeared. The folks adore the arrival thus of Muthumari Amman from India to dwell in their midst.

With the aid of artisans and craftsmen from India a nice temple has been erected for her, where she presides, bequeathing Grace.

Regular pujas are performed here and all Amman's special festival observances celebrated.

93. MUTHUMARI AMMAN KOVIL, MATALE

In the heart of Matale Town is a magnificent Hindu temple dedicated to Muthumari Amman. It is easily reached from the main road that runs through the town.

It is said to have been founded during the era of the Kandyan Kings by a venerable personage named Karuppannar. It was however built as a proper temple during the fifth decade of the last century by Suppiah Pillai to whom much credit is given. Since then several improvement works had been done and the temple today is most impressive with its mandapams, prahara and several other shrines, ornate pillars, covered and floored prahara veedy and many sculptural embellishments.

Though attributed by name to Muthumari Amman only, this temple is however comprehensively installed replete with all the divine forms of Hindu worship, thus becoming a popular sthalam where many devotees congregate.

Even as one enters the temple, the many shrines bewilder him with sanctifying devotion. There is an outside Vinayakar shrine and then the portal entrance Vinayaka and Palani Andavar shrines. Inside we worship the Pancha Maga Vinayaka Vigraham. The large Ranganatha deity is seen in a majestic setting accompanied by consorts Poothevi and Srithevi and others. The Nadaraja Murthi vadivam is seen accompanied by Sivakama Sunthari Ambal. The four Hindu saints (Nalvar) are there. The Siva Lingam elevates the temple to a Siva sthalam and the Devi Vigraham is Muthu Meenakshi Ambal. In the sanctum is installed a large vigraham of Muthumari Amman, serene and graceful.

The Navagraha shrine is in the western prahara; the Vigrahams and statutes installed are many, even those of Mathurai Veeran, Karuppannasamy and Kathavariyar have not been forgotten.

The temple and its temporalities are well managed by a devoted Trustee Board, which is responsible for the splendid organisation, especially at times of festivities.

Regular pujas are meticulously performed and the welfare of those who serve the temple is looked after. All the Hindu festivals are ceremoniously observed.

The Annual Mahotsava festival is in the month of February and lasts for 21 days. The Ther Chariot festival is truly a grand affair, lasting all night. The retinue is conveyed in five chariots, all towed by ropes by the devotees. Vinayakar occupies one chariot, Muthumari Amman in another, Somasuntheraswarer and Meenadshi in another, Subramaniar and his consorts in the next and finally the Chandeswari devotee in the last. The whole procession takes on a carnival like appearance during this annual feature when Sri Muthumari Amman bestows grace to her town folks of Matale and tharisanam to the thousands that gather there from all over the country.

94. MUTHUMARI AMMAN KOVIL, KOTAHENA, COLOMBO

A temple where devotees of different faiths seek the Divine Mother's Grace is this Muthumari Amman temple situated at Kotahena in Colombo North. Due to the crowded locality, the temple occupies only a small space.

As could be made out, if one were to listen to the names of upayakarar offering pujas and archanai chanted by the officiating priests, they come from many creeds, casts and walks of life. What force draws all these to the feet of the Divine Mother daily? Her benevolence must surely be magnanimous. I expect everyone has a grievance to be redeemed, a boon to be granted or a request to be fulfilled. Whatever that may be, thousands flock there and Amman's sannithanam is un-approachable due to thronging crowds on Tuesdays and Fridays. I have to avoid these days when seeking her tharisanam.

Muthumari Amman Kovil, Kotahena, Colombo Rajagopuram

Recently a Kumba abisheham ceremony was held on completion of improvements inside and the erection of a majestic gopuram at the entrance.

In the sanctum is the graceful Muthumari Vigrakam bequeathing tharisanam to all. Many Murthi Vigrakams in small little shrines enhance the temple which has a small inner prahara veedy also. On either side are the entrance (vasal) Vinayakar and Palani Andavar shrines.

In the praharam are shrines for Vinayakar, Vishnu, Kannakai Amman, Sivan and Parvathy and Subramaniyar deities, all facing east. In the northern praharam is the Nadarajah shrine and a shrine of the utsava amman. The simha nandi and palipedam are centrally installed.

A fairly large Ranganatha murthi in sayana pose, made in terra cotta, is placed together with consorts and attendants in an attic facing south.

Right at the entrance, a new right wing extension houses Nagathambiran, Saniyes-waran, Bhairavar and the Navagraha deities.

To the left of the entrance is the shrine room of Kali Amman. The new Amman Vigrakam is less fierce in appearance than the old huge frightening statue, now placed away. We see in terra cotta figures the story of the Kovilan Kannahai episode.

The origin of this Amman shrine commences in the year 1856, when some members of the Thiru vilanga nagarathar Chetty community brought some token soil from their village Erukankadi in Kovilpaddi Takuku in South India and commenced a simple shrine for Mari Amman at Kotahena, Colombo. Improvements and additions were completed later, on completion of which a Kumba abishekam ceremony was celebrated in 1954. Again, further improvements were done and thanks to N. Manoharan, architect and ardent devotee, a suitable Raja Gopuram was also erected at a cost of three and a half lakhs rupees.

Regular pujas and festivals are held as in agamic ambal temples. A large congregation of devotees throng the temple daily. They all seek Amman's Grace.

KANNAKAI AMMAN KOVILS

The Pattini cult in Lanka

The Pattini cult was introduced to ancient Lanka in the second century, when several temples were founded for the worship of Kannakai Amman.

The story of Kovilan and Kannakai has been immortalised in an ancient Tamil literary composition titled 'Silapadikaram' by Ilangovadikal. Ilango was a Tamil poet of Royal blood, being a brother of the Chera king Senkuttuvan (113-135 AC) who ruled at Thiruchchen Kottai, in the western coast of South India. The mighty king Senguttuwan established worship of Pattini Devi, with great pomp and glory in the second century. Neighbouring kings were all invited for the festive occasion to his capital city. A statue of the Devi, carved from a stone brought by the king from the Himalayas was ceremoniously consecrated thereby establishing worship of Kannakai Amman as a goddess. However the cult is not widely prevalent in India today.

King Gaja Bahu (111-135 AC) of Lanka, who was also present at the consecration brought with him to Lanka an emblem of the sacred 'anklet' of the Devi, gifted to him by Cheran Senguttuvan (ref 1), landing with this precious relic at the northern port of Samputhurai (Jambukola) it was placed on a caparisoned elephant and with many elephants following behind, a Royal procession was formed with flags and beating of drums. The procession wended its way, conveying the sacred relic, to several places in the Island. Wherever it halted, a temple for the worship of the Devi was founded. In fact, by Royal request, temples were erected all over the Island dedicated to her worship and the Pattini cult became established in Lanka. The cult spread far and wide and Pattini Devales and Kannakai Amman temples are found all over the Island particularly in the Eastern region.

Kannakai Amman Temples in the North:

There are yet several Kannakai Amman temples in the North, though many have changed and are now dedicated to the worship of Naga Ambal, Rajeswari Ambal, and Muttumari Amman. Kannakai amman temples are found today at Illavalai, Mandaitivu, Pallai, Veeman Kamam Tellipallai, Masiyapiddi, Kachchai, Pt. Pedro, Puloly and Karai Nagar. The first to be erected according to Mootoothamby's 'Jaffna History' is the temple at Velamparai Navatkuli. The Vattapalai Amman Kovil near Mullaitivu is a famous shrine which attracts large crowds during the annual festival. Local folk-lore is that Kannakai Amman personally visited this place. At Madduvil, the well known Panri thalachchi Amman Kovil reveres Kannakai Amman.

The origin of all Kannakai Amman Temples has to be attributed to the second century fervour to venerate the Pattini Devi.

Kannakai Amman Temples in the East:

Amman worship is widely prevalent in the eastern region of the Island. Rituals of worship adopted there are also unique in pattern. The temple at Karaitivu South of

Batticoloa is a foremost place venerated by everyone. Amman temples are also found at Amirthakaly, Muthalai Kuda, Kokkadicholai, Kalkudah, Mukathuvaram, Kannan Kuda, Eruvil nagar, Akkaraipattu Vallaichenai, Kal-munai, Thambiluvil, Vantharu moolai, Koyitpothivu, Ariyampathy etc; almost every place of some importance has an Amman Kovil.

At most of these, festivities are usually held once a year, only during this time the temple gets into proper function. The story of Kovalan and Kannakai is read and at some of them there is also a fire walking ceremony.

Reference:

1.   Raghavan, M. D. 'Tamil culture in Ceylon', p. 238

96. PANRI THALAICHCHI AMMAN KOVIL AT MADDUVIL

There is a story, prevalent locally, narrating an episode as to how the Kannakai Amman temple at Madduvil (near Chavakachcheri) became to be known as Panri Thalaichchi Amman Kovil.

A member, of the local community, had illicitly slaughtered another's goat. On becoming aware of the wrath of the owner, he had prayed to Kannakai Ammaiyar and entreated her aid to ward off the impending arrest and punishment. He had begged that the head of the goat be transformed to that of a wild boar (slaughter of which is free) and lo! At the time of inspection, to all appearances there it was, the head of a wild boar, and the devotee was declared innocent. People flocked to see the miracle and the temple became to be known accordingly.

The Ambal's miracle soon became known far and wide and all and sundry gather today at Ambal's feet, at Her humble shrine, seeking her aid. She is said to be very amenable and considerate.

The outstanding pongal day at the shrine is the full-moon day in the month of May, but nowadays every Monday, particularly in March are days for her worship. I have been able to bow in worship of the Ambal on several occasions when engaged in constructing the 'Separation Bund' of the Jaffna Lagoon scheme.

97. VATHTHAPALAI KANNAKAI AMMAN KOVIL, MULLAITIVU

Of the temples dedicated to Kannakai Amman, the Vaththapalai Amman Kovil, near Mullaitivu, is very well known. The site is filled with devotees who boil rice during the annual pongal night. The Vaththapalai Pongal is held on the full-moon day in May and is very largely attended by devotees particularly from the Vanni district. The month of May is a healthy month with monsoonal blowing; it is also the fruit season in the Northern Districts and is therefore an ideal month for Pongal ceremonies and offering of fruits.

With the onrush of more and more devotees who desire to boil the rice (Pongal), demands on the source of water supply exceeds the water feed to the Kerni which therefore becomes empty early in the evening. Devotees have to then eke out droplets from the springs that feed the Kerni.

This was the difficult problem that I was called upon to solve in 1949. Along with others, I walked up the valley, to the very source of the water resources of the valley, about a mile through paddy fields. There, an abandoned tank was found, conserving the entire flow of the valley, but lying in a breached condition. With the restoration of the breaches, the tank once again detains and stores the north-east monsoonal flow, feeding the springs all along the valley. For the success of the entire concept, storage in the tank should not be used up for Maha season cultivaton; cultivation here should be Manavari as originally intended to be. Then the detained-storage in the upper reaches of the valley would feed the springs that feed the Kerni near the temple and we can then enjoy Vaththa-Palai (a Kerni which does not go dry) conditions, for the pongal season even in the dry month of August.

Local legend is that Kannakai, on the conclusion of the Kovalan episode, left Madurai for Lanka. Arriving at Nainativu (Nagadeepa), she had stopped at various places, the tenth of which was Vaththapalai (thereby the location derived its name of paththam palai) where she performed her final ablutions to alleviate her karma. The place thus became an important place for her reverence. The munificence of visiting pilgrims from Madurai and that of the local Vanni chiefs enabled the erection of a temple structure and the building of the celebrated fresh water kerni in the ancient days. It is said that the temple was spared demolition by foreign invaders, who nevertheless destroyed other temples.

The festivities of the annual pongal, mentioned above, last a week. An unusual event is keeping a flame lit, burning bright on sea water (theertham).

98. ANGAN AMMAI KADAVAI KOVIL
Kadiramalai and Kanterodai

One of the earliest places of Kannakai amman worship, but which is now no more, was the temple for Pattini Theivam at Angan ammai Kadavai near the present village of Kanterodai, Jaffna; known as Kadirarhalai it was the seat of the Naga kingdom, Nagadeepa in the North. The place was especially receptive to King Gaja Bahu as his queen was a Naga Princess, daughter of Mahalteka Naga who ruled at Nagadeepa.

So, Kadiramalai would have put out its best in receiving the Royal procession of Gaja Bahu on its arrival from Sambuthurai, mentioned earlier. The festivities would have been on an elaborate scale culminating with the erection of a magnificent temple to Pattini Devi. Thus Kadiramalai acquired a sanctity which it preserved for several centuries.

'A colossal statue of a King', says Mudaliyar C. Rasanayagam (ref 1) 'is said to have been standing opposite to the temple of Kannakai at Anganammai Kadavai (Angana a goddess) near Kanterodai and broken by an elephant about a century ago. The feet and head of such a statue were found by Dr. P. E. Pieris in the premises of the temple and are now placed in the Jaffna museum. This statue was perhaps that of Gaja Bahu who after consecrating the temple for the worship of Kannakai placed his statue in front of it.'

A limestone sculpture showing feet with anklets found in the early Kanterodai excavation is among the collection at the Jaffna National Museum (ref 2).

Kannakai Amman Kovil, Anganammai

However, there is now at Mahiyapidde, a village close by, a temple known as Anganammai Kadavai Kovil, housing both a Kannahai Amman and a Meenadchi

Ambal Vigrahams. Originating as a simple shrine, after a vision of three maidens seeking solace in the area, it is now quite a medium sized temple where all traditional ceremonies and festivals are observed.

Angananimai Meenadchi Amman Kovil.

Across the road a Mari Amman temple has also been erected.

Kadiramalai

Early coins, punch marked coins or puranas, discovered by Paul E. Pieris during his excavations in 1918-1919, bear evidence of international trade here. As the seat of the Naga Kingdom it had been visited by celebrated personages. It has also been identified by some as the 'manipallavam' or manipuram of the Maha Bharata epic. It is also said that when the sapling from the sacred bo-tree was brought to Lanka, landing at Sambuthurai, the procession made a stay here and proceeded to Anuradhapura. Later the place became an important place of pilgrimage and many religious monuments were erected here.

Navaratnam C. S. 'Kanterodai' 1967:

'Describing the events at the end of the eighth century' writes C. S. Navaratnam, 'the Vaipava Malai, a chronicle of Jaffna says that in A. C. 795 Ugra Singan a Kalinga Prince made a descent upon Lanka with a numerous force from vadathesam (India). This Jaffna king ruled from Kadiramalai (Kanterodai).'

Kadiramalai becomes Kanterodai:

Kadiramalai, sacred to Kadiran, He who holds the lance (Vel), and malai, from where he bestows Grace to his devotees was the seat of the Naga Kingdom of the North for several centuries before and after king Vijaya. Centuries later, after the fall of that kingdom it had become referred to as Kandiragoda and later Kandergoda. During the Portuguese era it became Kandercude and eventually the Dutch made it Kantarodai, by which name we know it now.

Epitaph

A fitting epitaph to the glory of Kanterodai can be the following deduction by Dr. Paul E; Pieris (ref 3): 'Kanterodai has no reason to be ashamed of its contribution towards the increase of our knowledge regarding the ancient history of our Island .... I suggest that the North of Ceylon was a flourishing settlement centuries before Vijaya was born. I consider it proved that at any rate such was its condition before the commencement of the Christian era.'

That is the story of the many temples that were founded in ancient Lanka for reverence to a woman made Divine and who to this day is worshipped as Goddess Pattini Devi and Kannakai Amman.

Reference:

1.   Rasanayakam Madaliyar., 'Ancient Jaffna,' 1926, p 74

2.   Raghavan, M.D. 'Tamil Culture', p.94

3.   JCBRAS vol XXVIII No. 72, p 65

DRAUPATHAI AMMAN SHRINES

99. DRAUPATHAI AMMAN KOVIL, PANDIRUPPU, BATTICALOA

At Pandiruppu, a village North of Kalmunai in the Batticaloa District is the shrine for Draupathai Amman of the Maha Bharatham. The temple is said to have been erected by one Thathan, who came from North India. He erected the temple with assistance from Edirmanasingham, a local Chief and instituted the well known annual 'Theepallaium' festival. During the festival which lasts for eighteen days, in the month of August, the Maha Bharatam story of the Pancha Pandavar is recited culminating with a fire walking ceremony on the last day. Persons dressed up as Pancha Pandavar and Draupathai, lead by the Poosakar, walk slowly over red hot cinders, in a twenty foot long trough. The performance commemorates the purification ceremonies depicted in the original Puranam. After they have bathed in the sea, the purification is complete and many devotees seek holy ash from them as they are now blessed.

King Vimala Tharuma Sooriyan King of Kandy (1594-1604) is reported to have witnessed the festival and made a donation of paddy fields and other gifts for the maintenance of the temple.

Other temples in commemoration of Draupathai Amman are found in Batticaloa town (Puliyantivu) and at Palugama.

Reference:

Pandit V. S. Kandiah, 'Maddai Kalappu Thamilakam' (Tamil), 1964, p. 431

100. VISHNU TEMPLE AND DRAUPATHAI AMMAN KOVIL UDAPPU, PUTTALAM

Turning off at Battulu Oya junction, near the sixty-first milepost on the Colombo-Puttalam Road, and proceeding about four miles west, we reach the settlement of Udappu, by the seaside.

The friendly Udappu folks form a community by themselves. They are said to have migrated from their homeland in India during the era of King Bhuvenaha Bahu of Kotte. Dr. C. Sivaratnam writes; '.... they came with their servants, priests, flags and hereditary emblems of their clans'. Landing in Mannar they trekked southward and '.... finally settled down at Udappu and installed their Goddess Draupadi at Draupadi Devi Kovil'.

Draupathai Amman temple, Udappu
The temple of the friendly Udappu folks

The sandalwood image of the Amman was replaced in 1907 with a sculptured Vigraham in stone. A fundamental change was however made in 1912. As the main feature depicted at this temple was the Maha Bharata episode, it was considered desirable, on the advice of Sellapah Kurakkal, that Lord Krishna, the key personality of the Bharata wars should be given the main place in the temple. Draupathai Amman is housed in a special shrine in the artha Mandapam, facing South. Vinayaka and Muruka Murthies are also installed.

Along with the Nandi Devar a special feature is made depicting Veera Pathirar. A Raja Gopuram at the entrance and elaborately constructed vimanam over the Vishnu and Amman shrines add beauty to the temple. Ornamental pillars, and an embellished Mandapam, all impress the visitor that the temple is well supported by the devotees.

As Muthu Raman, a retired teacher and a leading devotee, explained to me when I went to make my obeisance to the Devi, every one there has a share in this, their Amman Kovil. Daily puja ceremonies are attended to by the priest, in the mornings and in the evenings. The temple impresses one as well supported and well built by devout devotees of the Devi.

Moolasthana Vimanam
The figures on top depict various Avatarams of Lord Krishna

The chief annual event is the ten day festival in August, which commences with the flag hoisting ceremony. The place assumes a carnival appearance at that time. Episodes from the Maha Bharatam, the story of the Pancha Pandavar are depicted as a pageant. The climax is reached with the fire walking ceremony on the last day which attracts large crowds from all over the Island.

There are also other temples in the Udappu settlement.

OTHER AMMAN KOVILS

101. NACHCHIMAR AMMAN KOVILS

Worship of the seven mothers or virgins, Saptha matricas or saptha Kannimar has been an ancient Hindu tradition. It is not known how it began; some believe that it may have developed from reverence to the six Kartikai Kannimar who suckled infant Skanda in the divine lake Saravana poikai. Others think that it grew from a purely tutelitarian concept confined to certain localities or groups. Anyhow the concept appears to be very flexible, permitting them to bear names, at one time associated with the high gods of the Hindu pantheon; from that exalted celestial status we find they also refer, at another time, to purely humans beset with the woes and griefs of the ordinary person.

However it may have originated, it has been an accepted system of religious worship among the ancient Hindus and in Lanka too, as Navaratnam states (ref 1) 'The worship of the seven goddesses (Nachchimar or Saptamatrikas) was also prevalent in ancient Ceylon. The energetic female principle of the Vedic gods constituted the Saptamatrikars. Temples dedicated to these goddesses were at Mannakandal between Odduchuddan and Puthukudiyiruppu'.

An interesting remnant of this worship is narrated by Navaratnam (ref 2). 'In the peninsula of Kalpitiya to the north of Pallivasathurai is a ruined tank with granite steps all around, the perimeter of this tank is about four miles. Ruined buildings are on all sides of the tank and the ruins on the western side look like those of a Hindu temple. A few icons still remain to remind us of its gloried past. The tank is called Nachchiamman Gangai and the temple is called Nachchiamman Kovil. There are many hallowed traditions about this temple and its thirtham'.

The institution of a Nachchimar kovil by tank or theertham, ruins of which are described above, has very likely been established in Lanka as had been prevalent in India. At Viragunar, about 10 km east of Madurai, by the south tank of river Vaikai, Prof. Bussabarger (ref 3) refers to seven virgins placed on a stacco base, being revered as tutelary deity of the water tank.

In the Vanni regions of Sri Lanka the myth of the seven Nachchimar has a local mundane association. The blessed seven are not so much the energetic principles of celestial gods as the valourous wifes of seven local Vanni chiefs (ref 4). These chieftains were defeated by the Hollanders and lost their lives in the battle field; so their wives ended their own lives by self-immolation, thus becoming deified as 'Veera Theivangal' and are revered by the Vanni folks as their tutelary deity.

Temples

Near Mullaitivu, is the ancient Vadduvakal Saptha Kannimar Kovil which gets into prominence during the festival at Vaththapallai Kannakai Amman kovil. The 'theertham' is taken on the first day from the former to the latter.

At Puttur East is a 'Veera Vani Saptha Kannimar Kovil'.

There are of course several Nachchimar Amman Kovils. They are to be found in Jaffna today at: Navaly, Chavakachchari, Neervely, Vellani, Saravanai and the Analaitivu island.

Some of the old Nachchimar Amman kovils are being changed to the worship of traditional agamic Ambal kovils.

I have not been able to collect information about the Eastern Province where this is known to be very prevalent.

References:

1.   Navarantam C.S.'Studies in Hinduism in Ceylon', p 4-5

2.   Navaratnam - 'Studies' p 86

3.   Bussabarger, Prof. Robert F. 'Splendours of Tamil Nadu', p.33

4.   Kanapathypillai Prof. 'Elathu Valvum valavum' (Tamil) p.48

102. SITA AMMAN KOVIL, NUWARA ELIYA

The Story of the Ramayana epic is well known to everyone. Sita Devi, the chaste wife of Sri Rama was abducted by Ravana, Emperor of Lankapuram, and kept in captivity until her release by Sri Rama and his vanara forces.

Sita Eliya in the outskirts of Nuwara Eliya along the road to Hakgalla is by legend associated with the Devi's stay in Lanka. 'Sita Eliya' (The plain of Sita), has been fittingly described (ref 1) as 'a charmingly undulating plain, fringed with thickly wooded hill sides, dotted with rhododendron bushes tipped with clusters of crimson flowers. Beyond are the steep mountain ramparts with the thickly wooded tops'. This is the legendary Asoka vanam, parts of which are traditionally perpetuated today as Hakgalla Botanical Gardens.

Pridham, the renowed historian gives a vivid description of the location and its legendary association (ref 2):

'In upper Ouva, adjoining the rocks of Hakgalla are the Nandanaodiyana (pleasure grounds) and Asoka Aramaya (Asoka Groves) of Ravana which are sanctified to Hindu Pilgrims by the events of the Ramayana and the traditions of Rama and Sita which are still preserved by the Brahmins of Kataragama. This district is included within the steep ranges of mountains in ancient legends called the walls of Ravana Garden which extended from Samanala to Hakgala and from Pedrutalagala to Gallegamma Kande. At the Northern end of the Hakgalla Mountains is the Seeth Talawa (Plain of Sita) where the goddess is said to have been concealed with Trisida, the niece of Ravana who was her sole companion. Hanuman, eluding the vigilance of the guards, contrived to penetrate to the bower and having delivered to Sita the Ring of Rama with assurance that her release would be effected, he proceeded to set fire to the neighbouring forests. It was this conflagration which cleared Nuwara Eliya and other plains in this region of genie according to the Hindoo and Cingalese legends and rendered them barren of useful production, in which state Vishnu has doomed them forever to remain'.

'A basin where the Sita Ella bursts from under the rock after an underground course of fifty yards is called the Seeta Konda. Here, round holes formed by the eddying streams are pointed out as the marks of the feet of the elephant ridden by Ravana when Seeta vanished and reappeared where the stream now does'.

This ella, which provides the name Sita Eliya to the place, is a brook of entrancing beauty. The perennial flow rushes by the rockside forming cascades making music, all its own. Here did, tradition says, Sita Devi spend her lone hours. Her ablutions and morning bath over, here she moaned for the speedy arrival of her Lord Sri Rama, in veneration and worship, for her liberation.

The Sita Amman Kovil found today at the site is but a humble tribute, in brick and mortar and tagaram sheets, perpetuating an immortal episode in the story of ancient Lanka. It was built by Sivamayam Sangara Swamy. The statues of Rama, Sita, Lakshmana, Hanuman, Krishna and Ganesh are found within.

Sita Amman Kovil, Nuwara Eliya
A humble tribute to an immortal episode in the annals of Lanka

The wild flower that is abundantly available in the region is the gloriously red coloured Rhododendron, known locally as 'Asoka mal' or popularly 'Sita mal'; one can well imagine these serving Sita Devi's puja devotions. Any way, it is 'Sita mal' today, and is seen wild in abundance, in this region, of over 5000 feet elevation.

This certainly is a place of serene reverence and the visitor seeks to offer a Sita - mal flower in homage to Sita Devi.

Reference:

1.   Raghavan, M.D., 'Ceylon a Pictorial Survey' 1962, p. 213

2.   Pridham, 'Ceylon and its dependancies' 1845 p. 23

SECTION VI

OTHER TEMPLES

103. NAGA THAMBIRAN TEMPLE AT NAGAR KOVIL, PALLAI

The Nagar Kovil Village

Nagar Kovil Village is a settlement, along the periphery of the Upparu Lagoon, situated about 12 miles from Pt. Pedro on the Chempiyyan Pattu Road. It is reached after passing Vallipuram Temple and Ampan Village. The settlement is extensive but sparsely populated. The people occupy themselves in paddy cultivation, coconut growing and in fishing for their livelihood.

Antiquarians agree that the Northern parts of Ceylon were, at one time, the seat of the Nagas. Mudaliyar C. Rasanayagam in his 'Ancient Jaffna' writes about it in detail and makes mention of Nagar Kovil being once the Head Quarters of the Naga Regime, and that even a big Nagar fort had existed close to the village. Ancient coins and pieces pottery have been picked up in the area.

The discovery of a golden plate, in 1953, close to Vallipuram Temple, making mention of Naga Regime, further establishes that the area was a prominent district of the Naga Province.

Such names as Chempian Pattu, indicate Chola influence and the subsequent Tamilian occupation of the area.

Naga Thambiran - the Deity of the Temple

The temple in Nagar Kovil village is a humble structure. The presiding deity of the temple is Naga Thambiran - the Supreme One or Siva held enclosed in her hood by the revered cobra. The Cobra was venerated by the ancients as representing Sakthi, i.e., Kundalini Sakthi. The name could also refer to the chief of or Thambiran of the Nagas. Siva has been referred to as 'Thambiran' by Saint Sekilar in his Periya Puranam. Pages of history thus get established of the Naga association with the locality and the Tamilian tribute for the sanctity of the place. Around the temple are four thirtha sites, each one for a specific cure. A plant peculiar to the place 'Sengnarai' flourishes here, which is believed to be a general cure for many ailments and a specific for snake bite.

Such a place, held in high reverence over two separate eras of civilization, through centuries, would no doubt have been a seat of divine manifestatian, working miracles.

The Kappal Thiruvila (The ship festival)

The annual festival at Naga Thambiran Temple at Nagar Kovil occurs in the month of October and lasts for ten days; of special mention is the seventh festival. On that night, the deity and the procession is halted in the third Prahara and we see enacted a performance depicting the advent of the Portuguese to the village in the 17th Century.

Traditon has handed down to posterity, a striking miraculous event in the history of the village. It is treasured by the village folks and is repeated annually.

Narrating the story of the folklore, recited in 'Virutham' style, partly dramatising it, the crowds that throng are told and they once again witness Nagammal - Naga Thambiran's protection of His people and the rescue of a thousand of the village youths.

The Portuguese territory in the Far East has been founded and to man these about a thousand youths were wanted by them for active service. The Portuguese arrive in their ships at Nagar Kovil - this time not for merchandise, bartering carpets or other ware for spices, but to requisition a thousand youths from that region. In the absence of volunteers, the armed might of the invaders drove a thousand youths from the village to the ship, to the dismay of the people of Nagar Kovil.

They were helpless against armed might and could only invoke their patron Protector Naga - Thambiran. Those were the days of faith and belief - to such only, miracles do occur.

The elements arose against the Portuguese - wind and storm - their ships were helplessly tossed about, and they could not leave the harbour and were fast sinking. At this stage, a cobra snake is seen on the top of the mast, scaring the Portuguese seamen who had gone up to heave the sails. Then lo! A person in frenzy tells the captain of the ship, that he must leave behind the Nagar Kovil youths if he is to set sail - such is the demand of the elements! When the snake was shot up into a thousand bits by the Portuguese, they came up as a thousand live snakes.

The captain is humbled and desired to yield but appeals as to how he was to identify the Nagar Kovil youths, from others they have herded into the ship's hold. He is told to look for a splash of powdered rice on their foreheads. Nagar Kovil youths would have a white Pottu.

Thus they were set free and set on land, even then one snake remained in the ship. The captain was told there was still one young maid whom a sailor held hidden in hold No.18, for housemaid service later. When she too was released, the storm abated. The Portuguese captain and sailors venerated the Nagammal - Thambiran Deity and sailed away, never to return.

Posterity commemorates the event with an annual thanksgiving festival observance, perpetuating the story of the miracle.

My obeisance to Nagathambiran was in Octber 1955, when I witnessed the Kappal - Thiruvila. As I had gone there in the company of my brother-in-law, who was the local District Medical Officer, I enjoyed a full and good view of what took place. I was able to take photographs and was later given a copy of the script of the dialogue.

104. AIYANAR TEMPLES

Aiyanar or Iyanar is the deity presiding over forests, tanks and fields. He safeguards agricultural activities. Shrines dedicated to his worship are found near paddy fields in the Vanni Districts. He carries in his hands the shepherds crook.

According to the Puranams, Aiyanar is the offspring of Shiva and Mohini. The form of Mohini was adopted by Vishnu to deal with Bhasmasuran, a demon.

Aiyanar is propitiated by the farmers during the cultivaton season, especially at times of drought. He safeguards the cultivation of the village folk, going about riding a horse, which often becomes the symbol for his worship, as is seen at Madampe, near Chilaw.

The steed provided to Aiyanar at Madampe
The author and his grandchild, are admiring it

The celebrated sculpture at Isurumuniya rock at Anuradhapura depicting a 'man and his horse' has been identified by some, as that of Aiyanar.

In the Sinhalese areas he is known as Aiyana and several Aiyana shrines are found in the Vanni Districts.

Among the shrines for Aiyanar in Jaffna are those at Varani, Arali and at Chunnakam. In the town itself, the Aiyanar Temple of Aiyanar Kovilady, Vannarpannai, has been dwarfed by the adjoining temple for Vinayaka Moorthi which has been renovated recently.

Entrance to Aiyanar Kovil, Madampe
The steed is seen in its stall on the left

The Aiyanar shrine near Vellankulam on the Mannar-Punakari Road is a stopping place for all travellers, where camphor is lit and coconuts broken for the worship of this pastoral deity.

At Periyakulam, a few miles from Trincomalee a large stone represents this divine guardian. Annually a pongal ceremony is observed by the cultivators near this Aiyanar stone.

There are several Aiyanar shrines in the Batticaloa District. In fact they are found in all the areas in Lanka, where the Vanniars settled during their era in early history.

In the Malayalam-Travancore areas of South India, he is known as Aiyappan. Thousands of devotees trek to Saverimalai hills, where according to legends, he had originated from the back of the right hand of Vishnu. So he is Keiyanar, and the elephant is his vahanam.

APPENDIX

CELEBRATED PATRONAGE OF HINDU TEMPLES

This appendix shows the involvement of various celeberated figures in the history of the island of Sri Lanka in many of the Hindu Temples described in this book. The chronology is approximate. There is an occasional reference to an alternate date. This is due to different sources giving different dates for the reign of the early Jaffna Kingdom.

Where possible reference is made to historical documents and the following key is used.

DKM   Dakshana Kailasa Manmiam

DKP   Dakshana Kailasa Puranam

YVM   Yalpana Vaipava Malai

AJ   'Ancient Jaffna' by Mudaliyar C Rasanayagam

KJ   'Kingdom of Jaffna' by S Pathmanathan

Ins   Stone Inscription

Tr   Temple tradition

R   Ramayanam

CS   CS Navaratnam

JPL   JP Lewis

DrPP   Dr Paul E Pieris

VP   Vishnu Puranam

CV   Culavamsa

CENTURY	ASSOCIATED PERSON	REGIME OR EPITHET	ACTION	NAME OF TEMPLE	LOCATION	REFERENCE	CHAPTER
Nebulous Epoch	Kethu Bhagavan			Kethu - Iswaran	Mannar	VP	30
	Maha Vishnu	Madiccha Avatharam		Vallipuram alvar Koyil	Vallipuram	DKM	73
	Maha Vishnu	Koorma Avatharam		Ponnalai Perumal Koyil	Sambuthurai	DKM	72
	Brahma			Muneswaram Temple	Chilaw	DKP	33
	Maha Thuradda	Viswakarma King Divine Architect	Founded	Thiruketheeswaram Temple	Mannar	DKM	30
24th - 15th century BC	Ravannan	Emperor of Lankapuranam	Founded	Koneswaram Temple	Koniamalai	R	31
	Rama Bhagavan	Rama Avatharam	Founded	Rama Linga Iswaram Temple	Manavenrawa	DKP	34
8th century BC	Agasthyar	Maha Munivar	Founded	Agastya Sthapanam Sivan Temple	Thiru Karasai	DKP & TKP	32
	Nagar Regime	Northern Kingdom	Founded	Thambakeswaram Naguleswaran Sivan Temple	Kadiramalai	YVM & AJ	38
			Founded	Nagathamburan Koyil	Nagar Koil	YVM & AJ	103
			Founded	Naga Pooshani Ambal Temple	Nagadipe	YVM & AJ	83
	Veddahs	Dwellers of the Eastern Region	Founded	Chitra Velautha Swamy Koyil	Verugal	Tr	59
			Founded	Kandaswamy Koyil	Mandur	Tr	61
			Founded	Chitra Velutha Swamy Koyil	Thiru Koyil	Tr	63
			Founded	Veluatha Swamy Koyil	Okanda	Tr	62
	Veddahs	Dwellers of the Southern Region	Founded	Kataragama Deviyo Temple	Kadirkamam	Tr	64

CENTURY	ASSOCIATED PERSON	REGIME OR EPITHET	ACTION	NAME OF TEMPLE	LOCATION	REFERENCE	CHAPTER
5th century BC	Vijaya (483 - 445 BC)	King of Lanka	Restored	Naguleswaram Temple	Keerimali	DrPP	38
			Restored	Koneswaram Temple	Koneswaram	DrPP	31
			Restored	Thiruketheeswaram Temple	Mannar	DrPP	30
			Restored	Thondeswaram Temple	Mantota	DrPP	
2nd century BC	Ellalan (204 - 160 BC)	Chola Prince	Founded	Varunikulam Sivan Kovil	Turukai		27
2nd century AC	Gaja Bahu	King of Lanka	Founded	Kannakai (Pathini) Amman Kovil	All Island		95
5th century AC	Chola Karikan 436 AC (another date 1223)	Chola Prince Kulakoddan	Restored	Koneswaram Temple	Koneswaram Koyil Kadavai	VVM & KJ	31
8th century AC	Maruthappiravalli	Chola Princess	Founded	Kandaswamy Temple	(Maviddapuram)	VVM	56
10th to 11th century AC	Chola Power in Lanka (985 - 1070)	Regime at Polannaruva	Founded	8 Sivan Temples	Janianada Mandalam		36
	Talikumaran	Chola Dignitary	Founded	Raja Rajeswaram Temple	Raja Raja Puram	Ins.	51
	Tevan Carittnian	Chola Dignitary	Founded	Tiru Viramewaram Temple	Raja Raja Puram	Ins.	52
	Karunakara Thondaiman	Chola Dignitary	Founded	Karunakara Pillayar Temple	Urumpirai	Ins. And Tr.	4
	Karunakara Thondaiman	Chola Dignitary	Founded	Selva Sannithy Temple	Thondaimannar	Tr.	57
	Virupaakhan	Merchant	Founded	Ithihadi Sivan Kovil	Charukachcheri	DKP	26
12th century AC	Parakrama Bahu I (1153 - 1255)	King of Lanka	Founded	13 Hindu Temples	All Island	CV	
	Parakrama Bahu I (1153 - 1255)	King of Lanka	Restored	103 decayed Hindu Temples	All Island	CV	

233

CENTURY	ASSOCIATED PERSON	REGIME OR EPITHET	ACTION	NAME OF TEMPLE	LOCATION	REFERENCE	CHAPTER
13th century AC	Kalinga Magha (1215-1255) Rules at Polannaruwa	Regime of the Northern Vanniyars	Restored	Thiruketheeswaram Temple	Matoddam	YVM, KJ & Tr.	30
			Restored	Pillaiyar Kovil	Athimoddai	Tr.	13
			Restored	Sivan Temple	Varunkulam	Tr.	27
			Founded	Than Thonni Iswaran Temple	Oddchuddan	Tr.	29
			Founded	Santhirasekaran Temple	Cheddikulam	IPL	14
			Founded	Sivan Temple	Pananikarnam	Tr.	28
			Founded	Uruthira Puram Sivan Temple	Kilinochchi		39
			Founded	Kasaturai Pillaiyar Temple	Kankesanturai		7
		Regime of the Eastern Vanniyars	Founded	Mamaga Iswara Pillaiyar Temple	Battcaloa	Tr.	15
			Founded	Than Thonnya Iswaran Temple	Kokkadicholai		37
			Restored	Kandaswamy Temple	Mandur		61
			Founded	Draupathai Amman Koril	Pathiruppu		99
13th century AC	Sundara Pandyan (1251 - 1280)	Pandya King	Restored	Konewaram Temple	Koneswaram		31

CENTURY	ASSOCIATED PERSON	REGIME OR	ACTION	NAME OF TEMPLE	LOCATION	REFERENCE	CHAPTER
13th century AC	Singai Ariyan (Kulangai) (soon after 1284 AC)	Ariyachakravarty King of Jaffna	Founded	Kailaya Nathar Temple	Nallur	YVM	2
			Founded	Saddanathar Kovil	Nallur	KJ	23
			Founded	Veyyil Ukanda Pillaiyar Temple	Nallur	KJ	16
			Founded	Veera Maha Kali Koyil	Nallur	KJ	90
			Founded	Thaiyal Nayaki Ambal Koyil			
			Founded	Salai Vinayakar Koyil			
14th century AC	Varotaya Singai Ariyan (about 1320) (Alternate date 1302 AC)	Pararajasekaram	Repaired	Several Temples	Kingdom of Jaffna	Tr.	
	Martanda Singa Ariyan (1356 - 1374) (alternate date 1325 AC)	Ariyachakravarti King of Jaffna	Repaired	Several Temples	Kingdom of Jaffna	YVM & KJ	
	Kuna Pushanan AC (alternate date 1342 AC)	Ariyachakravarti King of Jaffna	Founded	Perumal Koyil	Jaffna	YVM & CS	71
15th century AC	Kanaka Suwiyam AC (1440-1450)(alternate date 1410)	Sekarajasekaram	Restored	Several temples	Kingdom of Jaffna	Tr. & CS	
	Sempaha Perumal Sapumal (1450 - 1467)	Sangabodhi Bhuweenaha Bahu, rules at Jaffna	Founded	Kardaswamy Temple	Nallur	KJ	55
16th century AC	Kanaka Suciyam Singai Ariyan (1407-1478)	Pararajasekaram	Founded	Pararajaschara Pillaiyar Temple	Iruvil	Tr.	3
			Restored	Several Temples			
	Araiakesari	Soolar and Minister	Founded	Araiakesari Pillaiyar Temple	Neerreli	Tr.	5
	Sangili (1519-1564)	Sekarajasekaram	Founded	Poothadayar Temple	Nallur	YVM	90
18th century AC	Vaithalinga Chettiyar	Merchant	Founded	Vaitheeswara Sivan	Vannarpannai		22
20th century AC	Sir P. Ramanathan (1851 - 1930)	Knight	Restored	Ponnambalavaneeswaram Temple	Colombo		35

235

GLOSSARY

Abishekam	annointing
Abishekam Chanka	annointing using chanks
Abishekam Kumba	annointing or consecration
Agamas	saiva sidhanta texts
Agastiyar	a munivar
Aiyanar	a deity
Ambal	goddess
Amuthu	boiled rice
Annathanam	gift of food (rice)
Antralam	inner hall
Anugraham	bestow Grace
Arasan	King
Artha mandapam	inner hall
Aru	river
Anil	Grace
Asthi	ash relics
Avataram	incarnation
Avudaiyar	lower component of the lingam
Bajanai	religious recital
Bhairavar	a deity
Bhakthi	loving devotion
Chandeswarar	a disciple of Siva
Darshan	vision, revelation
Dakshana	South
Deepam	waving of lights
Devasthanam	abode of the Divine
Devale	temple
Garbagraham	Holy of Holies
Gopuram	temple tower
Kavadi	piously convey
Kerney	pool
Kodi sthampam	flag staff
Kurukkal	priest
Maha mandapam	large hall
Moolasthanam	sanctum
Moorthi,murthy	deity
Nadaraja)	
Nadaraser)	dance form of Siva
Natarajah)	
Nalvar	the four chosen Saiva Saints
Nandi	Shiva's disciple
Navagraham	the nine planets
Nayanmar	the 63 Saiva Saints
Palli arai	night chambers
Parivaraha	(see) prahara

Patiham	canto of verses
Peedam	seat
Poosari, Poshakar	officiating as priest
Praharam	circum ambient passage
Prasatham	puja offering
Puja	worship
Puranam	ancient narrative
Ratham	chariot
Sakkaram	a Vishnu symbol
Sannithanam	temple sanctum
Sivarathri	Shiva's night
Sthalam	ancient holy place
Sthoopi	upper portion of vimanam
Thandikai	a decorated conveyance
Thanthonriya	appear by itself
Thapas	ascetic practices
Tharisanam	vision, revelation
Theepam	waving of lights
Theertham	holy water (unguent)
Thevaram	inspired hymns
Ther	a well constructed chariot
Therppai kulam	temple tank
Tiru	sacred
Unjal	swing
Utsavam	festival
Veedi	praharam
Villu	a swamp
Vimanam	tower over sanctum
Vigrakam	symbolic figure
Virutham	verse

About the Author

Sanmugam Arumugam, B.Sc.(Lond.), B.Sc.(Eng.), F.I.C.E.,F.I.E., was born in 1905, in Jaffna, Sri Lanka. Graduating in Engineering from King's College, London, he was an Irrigation Engineer for over thirty years. Ruins of many historic sites and ancient temples were visited when he had to visit irrigation works for restoration.

On retirement he wrote about Hindu Temples. He made a tour visiting the Hindu Monuments of ancient Java, and Hindu Agamic Temples of Bali and Lombok.

He passed away in 2000.

His other works:

Lord of Thiruketheeswaram
Koneswaram
Lombok and Its Temples
Stone Sculptures in Colombo Hindu Temples
Dictionary of Biography of the Tamils of Ceylon

Other books from Ohm Books Publishing

Tamils in Sri Lanka
A Comprehensive History (C. 300 B.C - C. 2000 AD)
Dr Murugar Gunasingam

Tamil Words for Travellers
Everyday words for visitors to Sri Lanka
Seggy & Jane Segaran

Peoples and Cultures of Early Sri Lanka
A Study Based on Genetics and Archeology
Dr Siva Thiagarajah

The Evolution of an Ethnic Identity
The Tamils of Sri Lanka (C. 300BCE to C. 1200 CE)
K Indrapala

Endless Inequality
The Rights of Plantation Tamils in Sri Lanka
Yogeswary Vijayapalan

Sri Lankan Tamil Nationalism
A Study of its Origins
Dr Murugar Gunasingam

Writings and Musings
Being a Collection of Articles Published in the Ceylankan
The Journal of the Ceylon Society of Australia
Thiru Arumugam

More information on these and other publications on Sri Lankan Tamil history and politics is available on the Ohm Books website. They are all available through Amazon and other on-line booksellers.